J. Gera

The RISE and FALL of the

CONSERVATIVE RESURGENCE

The Southern Baptist Convention: 1979-2021

TRUSTHOUSE
PUBLISHERS

Printed in the USA
First Edition, First Printing, 2021
ISBN: 978-1-945774-65-2

Trust House Publishers

P.O.Box 3181

Taos, NM 87571

www.trusthousepublishers.com

Ordering Information: Special discounts are available on quantity purchases by churches, associations, and retailers. For details, contact the publisher at the address above or call toll-free 1-844-321-4202.

1 2 3 4 5 6 7 8 9 10

PREFACE

THIS BOOK IS NOT INTENDED TO BE A COMPREHENSIVE recounting of the Conservative Resurgence in the Southern Baptist Convention in the last decades of the 20th century. James C. Hefley in his five-volume compendium: *The Truth in Crisis: The Conservative Resurgence in the Southern Baptist Convention,* Jerry Sutton in his book, *The Baptist Reformation: The Conservative Resurgence in the Southern Baptist Convention,* Paul Pressler in his book, *A Hill on Which to Die: One Southern Baptist's Journey* and other authors have covered the subject well.

While I want to review some of the concerns I had about Southern Baptists' drift into theological liberalism and highlight the gratitude I will forever have for those dear soldiers of the cross who "contend(ed) earnestly for the faith which was once for all delivered to the saints" (Jude 3); I also want to point out that without constant vigilance there is always the temptation to drift away from the belief that the Word of God is infallible. There is the natural inclination to depart from the truth and accept the deceitful and pretentious ideologies inspired and fueled by the Prince of this World.

Colin Cutler, a pilot, graphic designer and Boldmethod Co-founder, asserts that airplanes have left-turning tendences during takeoff. If you fly a lot perhaps you have felt like your plane was veering to the left edge of the runway on takeoff. There are four things that contribute to this phenomenon: (1) torque, (2) asymmetric propeller loading, (3) gyroscopic precession, and (4) spiraling slipstream. I actually don't understand any of that, but Cutler explains, "The four left-turning tendences create the forces that make your airplane veer left during takeoff. Step on the right rudder to cancel them out, and you'll maintain a perfect centerline throughout your takeoff roll."[1] I am convinced that without every precaution and without a faithful adherence to the Word of God, the same thing can happen to our theology. It will veer to the left.

Solomon, the wisest man in the Old Testament, who wrote Ecclesiastes, penned, "The heart of the wise inclines to the right, but the heart of the fool to the left" (Ecclesiastes 10:2 NIV). Here Solomon says folly is derived from a fault in the heart. A wise man's heart directs him towards the right, but a foolish man's heart directs him towards the left. While it is tempting for those of us who are more politically conservative to see this as a very prophetic insight from Solomon on how you should vote in elections, it is doubtful that the wise king was thinking in those terms. However, I think Solomon sees the heart as the seat of our emotions, affections and desires as well as the headquarters of our mental, moral and thinking processes. The wise man's heart will lead him to a place of honor, protection and favor, whereas the fool's heart will lead him astray.

---

1   https://www.boldmethod.com/learn-to-fly/aerodynamics/why-
     -you-need-right-rudder-on-takeoff-to-stay-on-the-centerline/
     Accessed March 23, 2021.

Today, there seems to be a dramatic shift to the left in evangelicalism in general and the Southern Baptist Convention in particular and the shift appears to have much more to do with the sufficiency of the Bible than the infallibility of the Word of God. In the last half of the 20th century Southern Baptists fought for the infallibility of Holy Scripture, because of a strong and unwavering conviction that the Bible is never wrong, and thus absolutely trustworthy and free from error. In II Timothy 3:16 the Apostle Paul wrote: "All Scripture is given by inspiration of God." We believe that God is infallible and thus incapable of giving us a written Word that is untrue or erroneous.

The sufficiency of Scripture means that we do not need 67 books in the Bible; and we don't need new revelation today to unveil the pathway to salvation and equip believers for Christian service. Christians don't need secret knowledge, special insights, cultural wisdom, political agendas or mystical experiences in order to know for certain that God exists, that Jesus, His Son, was born of a virgin, lived a virtuous life, died a vicarious death and rose victorious over death, hell and the grave and that the Holy Spirit was given to indwell us, empower us and seal us until the day of redemption. However, in the 21st century we are witnessing a strange and sad departure from the once firm position of the sufficiency of God's Word.

When a Convention President writes that Christians and Muslims worship the same God, when certain leadership promotes Social Justice, Critical Race Theory and Intersectionality, when it appears that voices in the Convention are softening their stand on homosexuality and beginning to embrace egalitarianism, when relativism, subjectivism, pragmatism and socialism are surreptitiously creeping into the churches of our denomination the question is this: Is there a way back?

"Yes, indeed"! I would like to think that there is a way back for those churches and for our denomination that seems to have retreated or turned away from the sufficiency of the Word of God? I think it is fairly late in the game and I am of the sincere belief that God would be justified in unleashing His judgment upon our denomination at any moment. For the most part we have dismissed Jehovah God from our public schools, our marketplaces, our political arenas, our entertainment and embraced a cultural Christianity that is as far from spiritual surrender as a monkey is from becoming the valedictorian of an Ivy League university.

However, I do have hope for another Conservative Resurgence, and more importantly, a spiritual awakening, because more than once God has stayed His hand of judgment and provided mercy and healing to individuals, churches and nations that returned to God with prayer, fasting, repentance and surrender. The city of Nineveh was filled with a wicked and recalcitrant people, but God reached down in mercy and preserved the city.

In the last chapter of this book we will take a brief look at the seven churches in Revelation 2-3, consider their weaknesses and strengths and discover that no matter how glaringly debilitating their weaknesses and how incredibly fragile their strengths the Lord of the Lampstands and the Christ of the Candlesticks urges them to "overcome." I don't believe our wonderful Saviour is given to offering false hopes and vain promises in order to have us chase rainbows and invest our lives in impossibilities . And yet to each of these churches the Lord offered hope when he said, "He that overcometh. . . ." Even though these churches were plagued with many liabilities and beleaguered with sins, the Lord Jesus gave them encouragement and the hope that they could "overcome" and be restored and revived.

We have an amazing group of young leaders in the Southern Baptist Convention who have the energy, passion and determination to help us refocus on the sufficiency of Scripture, the basics of evangelism, a renewed emphasis on revival and bring about the kind of changes that can help us overcome the current malaise and decline in our beloved denomination. This wonderful reality and the truth that God is immutable and just as powerful as ever gives me great hope.

TABLE OF CONTENTS

CHAPTER 1

THE HEART CRY FOR THE CONSERVATIVE RESURGENCE

SOUTHERN BAPTISTS, THE LARGEST EVANGELICAL denomination in the United States, have accomplished much for the Lord's work through the years of its existence. Large churches with spires that extend toward heaven have signaled a significant spiritual presence in metropolitan areas across the landscape of America. Suburban churches have lifted high the banner of Christ in sprawling neighborhoods from Virginia to California. Churches in small towns have been the centerpiece of their communities and have helped to keep the fires of our faith burning brightly. Faithful believers in rural churches – the kind of churches that gave birth to our denomination – have continued to keep the light of the Gospel burning despite many neighbors migrating to the large cities. Ethnic congregations have become a vital part of Southern Baptist life for which the faithful are forever grateful.

Baptist history has certainly had its share of glorious successes and pinnacle moments of divine prosperity. We must never forget that Roger Williams came to America from England to escape religious persecution and in 1638 established the First Baptist Church on this continent in Providence, Rhode Island. From that humble, but noteworthy beginning, the number of Baptists began to grow in America.By 1750 the expansion of Baptists in America was further fueled by the Great Awakening, pioneered by Jonathan Edwards and George Whitefield. Shubal Stearns, a colonial evangelist and preacher during the Great Awakening, took his Baptist beliefs from Connecticut to North Carolina in the mid-eighteenth century, planted a church in Sandy Creek, Guilford County, and inspired the establishment of churches across the state and beyond.

Amidst some of Baptists most blessed seasons of ministry and missionary endeavors, formidable challenges and daunting adversities have arisen. Individual churches would sometimes allow small grievances to boil over into serious conflicts that resulted in church splits. In addition to these local challenges, our history also reveals that there have been major conflicts that have created schisms in our broader Baptist family.

BAPTISTS CONFLICTS ARE NOTHING NEW

Charles Darwin's theory of evolution was first taught in the public schools of America in the years immediately following WWII, but the spiritual erosion of the Christian faith began during his lifetime (1809-1882). Many concluded that his *Origin of the Species*, published in 1859, disproved the Bible. They claimed that the Bible did not need to be correct in matters of science and history, because it was just a book of religion. In much of the academic world Darwin was authenticated and the Word of God was denigrated. Darwinism and theological liberalism began to spread throughout Europe from Germany into England in the 19th century. The impact of theological liberalism was devastating to the churches, because when the Bible is discredited the primary component of the church begins to wither and the result is catastrophic.

The deteriorating condition of the church in England prompted London Pastor Charles Hadden Spurgeon to write in the November 1887 edition of the *Sword and Trowel*, "Attendance at places of worship is declining and reverence for holy things is vanishing. We solemnly believe this to be largely attributable to the skepticism which has flashed from the pulpit and spread among the people." It was during this time that the Downgrade Controversy emerged, and Metropolitan Tabernacle departed from the local Baptist denomination, the Baptist Union in England. The Baptist Union tried to make peace by adopting a compromise doctrinal statement, but it was an anemic and inadequate attempt to sufficiently honor God's Word and created a deeper chasm between the few who stood with Spurgeon and the vast majority of those in the Baptist Union.

Dr. Jason Allen, President of Midwestern Baptist Theological Seminary, wrote a blog entitled *Spurgeon and the Downgrade Controversy* on December 21, 2015, stating, "Indeed, Spurgeon has been vindicated. The British Baptist Union is a shadow of its former self. Moreover, Spurgeon's Downgrade foreshadowed the Fundamentalist/Moderate

Controversy of the 1920s and the great SBC Controversy at the end of the 20th century. Doctrinal decay always brings dire consequences; the controversy cost Spurgeon dearly. In less than five years from the controversy Spurgeon would die at a relativity young late. Against his previously stated wishes, his supporters erected a massive burial tomb in the Norwood Cemetery. Ensconced on the front of it, beneath the marble replica of his likeness, is a marble Bible, opened to II Timothy 4:7 – 'I have fought the good fight, I have finished the race, I have kept the faith.'[2]

In the 19th century a multiplicity of differences was present in America and the influence of liberalism was already being felt in the churches of the land. Baptists in the South met May 8-12, 1845 in Augusta, Georgia to form the Southern Baptist Convention. Robert A. Baker, writing an article on Southern Baptist beginnings, explained that Baptist leaders, "recognized that there were numerous social, cultural, economic, and political differences between the businessmen of the North, the farmers of the West, and the planters of the South. These differences had already brought much rivalry between the several sections of the new nation. Each section continued to revive old colonial disagreements and wrestled with questions about how the new constitution should be interpreted, what constituted the final legal power, and similar problems.

"Perhaps most critical of all was the slavery issue. This practice had been forced upon the colonies by England early in the seventeenth century against the protests of Northerners and Southerners. Northern merchants, however, soon sought the profit involved in importing slaves from Africa. Southern

---

2   https://jasonkallen.com/2015/12/spurgeon-and-the-downgrade-controversy/ accessed February 5, 2021.

planters, the only ones able to use large numbers of unskilled laborers on large plantations in a relatively warm climate, helped to prolong this evil. At the height of this system, however, two-thirds of the white families of the South owned no slaves at all, and Baptists (who were generally of the lower economic status) were probably less involved than this."[3]

There were those, like missionary statesman Adoniram Judson, who tried to minimize the separation of Southern Baptists from the Northern Baptists by suggesting that there could be no harm in establishing another strong missionary society. However. H. Leon McBeth, author of *The Baptist Heritage*, in writing about the founding of the Southern Baptist Convention stated, "If (Judson's comments were) true in 1845, those hopeful sentiments were less true by 1900. Regional isolation, war bitterness, and differing emphasis in theology created chasms by the end of the century which leaders of an earlier generation could not have anticipated."[4]

Another Baptist brouhaha emerged after World War I when Southern Baptists attempted to establish fraternal relations with Baptists world-wide. Prior to the 1950s, Baptists were largely anti-ecumenical, and so any fraternal relationships outside the closest of the Baptist family was controversial. At first it appeared that some progress was being made in creating a collegial relationship with other Baptist groups, but it ultimately became what Tom Nettles called a "confessional firestorm." [5] When Baptist in the South expressed concern that modernism

---

3   While Baker's view may be out-of-favor in many circles, he aptly describes the tensions of the day.

4   Dr. H. Leon McBeth, The Baptist Heritage, (Nashville, Tennessee, Broadman Press, 1987, p. 392-393)

5   https://founders.org/2018/10/10/the-1925-baptist-faith-and-message-finding-a-rock-in-a-storm/ Accessed March 23,2021

had crept into denominational life in both the North and the South it began to become apparent that a consensus was more improbable than anyone could have anticipated.

BAPTISTS AND THEIR CONFESSIONS OF FAITH

By 1925 the need to reaffirm Baptist principles and practices attracted favorable attention and at the annual meeting in Memphis, Tennessee, Southern Baptists adopted its first formal confession of faith, called *The Baptist Faith and Message.* First Baptist Church of Fort Worth Pastor J. Frank Norris, sometimes called Southern Baptists' "most troublesome fundamentalist," led the charge to have a strong confession of faith alleging that biological evolution and modernistic views of Scripture were being taught in Baptist colleges and seminaries. [6] That trend apparently continued unchecked for decades.

In 1957, as a Royal Ambassador (a missions education organization for boys that was a part of life for almost every boy in the SBC at the time), I was selected to serve as a page at the North Carolina Baptist Convention. I recall several controversial issues that attracted my attention and introduced me to the fact that Baptists sometimes are divided by principles and practices. It was at that annual session that North Carolina Baptists reaffirmed its ban on campus dancing at their Baptist institutions of higher learning, which dated back to 1937. In the days that followed, Wake Forest students protested the decision by doing the bunny-hop and burning in effigy the president of the N.C. Baptist Convention, the Reverend J. C.

6   McBeth, op. cit. p. 677

Canipe. At that same convention there were a large number of Baptists who expressed their consternation over the fact that Wake Forest President Harold Tribble wanted to "modernize" the College board of trustees by allowing non-Baptists to sit on the Board. As innocuous as those issues may have seemed to some, others saw them as a "slippery slope" slanted toward liberal ideologies and practices. Even as a teenager I agreed with the conservative group of Baptists. In fact, I so admired Dr. Canipe, that he was the one I invited to preach in the first church I was called to serve as pastor.

It would be impossible to site every debate and controversy that has erupted in Southern Baptist life, but the dispute that erupted at Midwestern Baptist Theological Seminary in 1961 when Ralph Elliott, the chair of the Old Testament Department, authored *The Message of Genesis* should be noted. The commentary, published by Broadman Press, ignited the ire of a great number of Baptists from every clime and sector of the nation. The book focused on the higher-critical method of biblical interpretation and was considered to be an example of the teaching characteristic of other Southern Baptist seminary professors at that time. Current MBTS President Jason Allen indicated that Elliott's book "revealed beliefs (that were) out of sync with the vast majority of Southern Baptists." He added, "To be sure, Elliott's book was simply the match that ignited the flame. The tinder had been piling for some time. . . . However, it was K. Owen White's widely distributed article, 'Death in the Pot.' That landed like a bombshell in Kansas City and sent shockwaves throughout the entire convention. White argued Elliott's book was 'liberalism, pure and simple,' and, if left unchecked, would bring the denomination ruin."

McBeth explains that in 1962 a group of "Concerned Baptists" from Eight states met in Oklahoma City to plan a strategy to push the SBC rightward. Although their immediate purpose was to remove Elliott, their coming together reinforced the emerging conservative movement and convinced them they could, by careful strategy and persistent efforts, gain control of the convention and its agencies.[7] At the SBC annual session that same year White made a motion for the messengers to "affirm their faith in the entire Bible as the authoritative, authentic, infallible Word of God" and for the Sunday School Board to discontinue the printing of *The Message of Genesis*.[8] The motion to cease the printing of the book failed, but it may have prompted SBC President Hershel Hobbs to lead in the revision of the 1925 *Baptist Faith and Message,* which happened in 1963.

EXPOSED TO LIBERALISM

I had studied Baptist history in Training Union (a once-strong movement in SBC churches to train church members in issues of doctrine, history, and church polity), but I was mostly oblivious to all of the convention controversy as a child and teenager. I grew up in the foothills of western North Carolina. My grandfather, M. I. Harris, was my first pastor. He was a passionate preacher and known as a man of prayer. I grew up in a family that had an uncompromising allegiance to the Word of God. I was called to preach as a teenager. I went to Mercer University in Macon, Georgia, to prepare for the ministry, believing that it would be four years of spiritual education, heavenly inspiration and insightful revelation.

---

7   https://founders.org/2013/10/01/the-deterioration-of-the-baptist-
    -faith-and-message/Accessed March 23, 2021

8   https://archive.org/details/tellingstorieshi00rags p.33-37/Accessed
    March 23, 2021

In my first week on campus my faculty advisor asked me, "What do you want accomplish in the next four years – what is your chosen career path?"

I explained that I intended to prepare myself to be a pastor and study the Bible. The faculty advisor explained, "Well, if you are going to be a pastor you will need to go to a seminary when you finish your college education. That is where you will get your theological education. So, I would suggest that you take some religion courses here, but that you major in philosophy or English literature. I would suggest that you take German, because all the great theologians you will be studying are of German origin."

I decided to major in English literature, minor in history and study German as I had been advised. In the few religion classes I took I learned about the German theologians and their historical-critical approach to biblical interpretation. I became familiar with Paul Tillich, Gunther Bornkamm, Rudolf Bultmann, and brothers Richard and Reinhold Niebuhr, who were Americans with German origins. I studied Bultmann's method of demythologizing the Scripture and could not believe that learned professors seemed fascinated with the idea of deconstructing the Word of God. I was more than disappointed. I was actually devastated.

In a New Testament survey course, I heard a chilling example of demythologizing. The professor took one of Christ's greatest miracles, the feeding of the 5,000, which appears in all four Gospels; and he made an effort to rationalize it into something that could be understood in simple, human terms that required nothing of the supernatural. He explained that Jesus had been teaching the people until late in the day and the people were hungry.

The professor explained that one little boy could not wait any longer to eat and reached into his garment and pulled out the lunch his mother had prepared for him – two fish and five loaves (wafers). The people nearby saw him eating his lunch and because of his example, they too retrieved their lunches from their garments, and everyone had plenty to eat. However, the professor explained there was no miracle other than the boy's action emboldening the crowd to do what he did – eat what they had brought to what the Gospels describe as "a lonely place." I dismissed the professor's lecture that day as no more than the fanciful explanation of a liberal teacher enamored with his own intellect.

Some of our chapel services at Mercer seemed to be designed to challenge our faith rather than reinforce it. I think it was in my freshman year, when I was trying to fit into my new environment; and when I was most impressionable and vulnerable to all the new theological concepts, that we had our Religious Emphasis Week. Dr. Warren Carr, pastor of Watts Street Baptist Church in Durham, North Carolina was the speaker for the week. The history of his church states: "It was the feisty, independent Warren Carr who brought the Watts Street Baptist Church into being as an innovative, open, liberal church in the new South."

The church's history also explained, "He was a leader of the battle within the Baptist denomination to be more open both theologically (he opposed the literal interpretation of the Bible) and administratively (he favored abandoning the requirement of immersion for membership for those already baptized). During Carr's ministry the church had dual membership with the SBC and the American Baptist Convention and approved the ordination of women as pastors and deacons. [9]

9   James C. Hefley, The Truth in Crisis, Vol I (Dallas, TX, Criterion Publications, 1986, p. 44)

During the Religious Emphasis Week Carr sounded like he had read or perhaps co-authored Joseph Fletcher's book on *Situation Ethics* before it was published, because his messages were peppered with statements that sounded like they were taken from a new morality handbook. I think he may have been a proponent of the sexual revolution of the 1960s. He avowed that truth is relative and that love trumps all the laws that have been born out of Christian legalism. I could not embrace the new morality, because I had heard Billy Graham say, "The new morality is nothing but the old immorality." However, I felt like Carr's messages were giving the Mercer students the right to explore territory that had been previously banned and forbidden.

My experience at the seminary in the mid 1960s was no better. I had three professors who appeared to be strong in their convictions and helped to fortify my faith, but most of the others could be called what our Bible inerrancy champion, Dr. W. A. Criswell, referred to as pedagogues with "an opprobrious epithet" – or downright liberal. On one occasion we were in chapel and the students had been bombarded with so much neo-orthodoxy and higher criticism of the Holy Scriptures that when the chapel speaker/professor for the day said something that pierced the souls of those who had an uncompromising allegiance to the Word of God one student actually tore just a few pages out of his Bible, held up those pages in his hand, ran out of the chapel, lamenting and crying, "This is all of the Bible I have left."

Because my grandparents and parents had taught me to have an unapologetic love for the Word of God and because I knew the church I was pastoring would not accept the spurious theology that I was being taught, I was able to survive my formal higher education with my fundamental belief system intact. However, many of those who set out to become pastors, missionaries and church staff members abandoned their perceived calling somewhere along the way and left the seminary confused and groping for a sense of purpose in life.

Their lost sense of calling reminded me of John Steinbeck's book, *The Grapes of Wrath*. In the book Steinbeck tells about a preacher by the name of Jim Casey. He was a mixture of the goodness of Jesus Christ and the weakness of the common man. In the course of the book Casey began to have doubts about God, Jesus, the afterlife and the content of the Bible. In a condensed play of *The Grapes of Wrath* Casey is passing by a house and the people sitting on the front porch of the house ask Casey, "Hey, ain't you the preacher?"

He responds, "No, I ain't the preacher. I ain't sure what day it is; and I ain't sure about the weather. I am not even sure where my next meal is coming from; and when you ain't sure about nothing, you can't be no preacher." I felt like those thoughts should also be true of college and seminary professors.

James C. Hefley in Volume I of his *Truth in Crisis* series of books recalls a lecture that Chauncey R. Daley delivered in a Southern Seminary classroom. Daley, described by Hefley as "a leading ideologue of the SBC moderates", exclaimed, "Doctrinally or inerrancy wise, the poison (conservatives) claim is Biblical criticism. That's what they are after. . . When the seminaries started teaching Biblical criticism and started talking about documentary hypothesis and other conclusions, that's when the poison started. I can remember one professor who stood up strongly for the Mosaic authorship of the Pentateuch. . . The seminaries have been moving in that direction . . . If you want the Mosaic authorship of the Pentateuch, the historicity of the first eleven chapters of Genesis, and Job and Jonah as historical figures, go to Mid-America." [10]

GOING TO THE SOUTHERN BAPTIST CONVENTION

I went to my first Southern Baptist Convention annual meeting in 1968 in Houston. Dr. Martin Luther King, Jr. had been assassinated just two months prior to the annual session and racial tension was high. Bobby Kennedy, who had just won the South Dakota and California presidential primaries in his run for the U. S. presidency, was mortally wounded by Sirhan Sirhan at the Ambassador Hotel in Los Angeles during the course of the SBC meeting in Houston.

Aside from adopting a resolution on violence, including "the lynching, rioting, burning, and shooting" prompted by the assassinations of Robert Kennedy and Dr. King and a straw vote to see if there was sufficient interest in changing the name of the SBC, the annual meeting was relatively calm. H. Franklin Paschall, pastor of First Baptist Church in Nashville, TN, was president of the Convention, but according to James C. Hefley, Paschall "could overlook neo-orthodoxy, but neither (he nor his predecessor, Wayne DeHoney) were believed to personally hold the position that only the message of Scripture was infallible." [11]

It was at the Houston annual meeting in 1968 that W. A. Criswell, pastor of First Baptist Church in Dallas, Texas, was elected to his first term as president of the Southern Baptist

---

10   Ibid., p. 52

11   https://wacriswell.com/sermons/1985/whether-we-live-or-die-sbc/
Accessed March 23, 2021

Convention. The election of this great preacher, the likes of which we have not seen in our present generation, was not the beginning of the Conservative Resurgence, but it signaled the birth of a new era in Southern Baptist life. His book, *Why I Preach the Bible Is Literally True*, published by Broadman Press in January of 1969, provided Southern Baptists with a persuasive testimony to the absolute infallibility of the Bible.

Almost two decades later, at the Pastor's Conference prior to the Southern Baptist Convention in Dallas in 1985, Dr. Criswell preached his message entitled Whether We Live or Die. The passionate preacher tossed restraint to the four winds and hurled his grenades of truth to an enormous audience that had packed and jammed every nook and cranny of the vast Dallas Convention Center. If ever a preacher spoke straight from his heart, W. A. Criswell did that night. Using the brush of a skilled artist with dexterity and mixing his colors with the skill of one who knows his craft, he painted word pictures that are still embedded in the memory of those who heard him on that unforgettable night. In his own inimitable way, he thundered, "No minister who has embraced a higher critical approach to the gospel has ever built a great church, held a mighty revival, or won a city to the Lord. They live off the labor and sacrifice of those who paid the price of devoted service before them. Their message, which they think is new and modern, is as old as the first lie, "Has God indeed said?" (Genesis 3:1-KJV).[12]

Dr. Criswell said that he first heard about the theological crisis in the Convention, and the methodology that could be implemented to correct it, in October 1978 and would have initiated a plan to begin to resolve the matter during his SBC

---

12   Judge Paul Pressler, A Hill on Which to Die, (Nashville, Tennessee, Broadman and Holman Publishers, 1999, p. 95)

presidency if he had only known how pervasive the problem had become.[13] Nevertheless, his influence and support of the Conservative Resurgence was invaluable.

The Conservative movement was carefully crafted by knowledgeable architects who developed a proposal that was conceived in prayer and designed with understanding. To most active Southern Baptist church members the names of Paige Patterson and Paul Pressler have been attached to the conservative fight for the inerrancy of the Bible in Southern Baptist life. They understood the formula provided by the Southern Baptist Convention's Constitution and By Laws that would provide for a logical and responsible method for changing the theological trajectory of the denomination; and Southern Baptists are indebted to them for their heroic leadership and sagacious plan to craft a needed change in direction for the SBC. However, there were other, perhaps lesser-known individuals, who were also champions in the battle for Biblical fidelity.

Since I grew up as a Tarheel and married a Georgia peach and served the Lord in Georgia longer than in any other state, there are two men who stand out in the battle for the Bible from my somewhat limited perspective. In North Carolina, Dr. M. O. Owens, Jr., pastor of Parkwood Baptist Church in Gastonia from 1963 to 1980, was a champion of Biblical inerrancy. He lived to be 105 years old. He was born in New Holland, South Carolina on September 4, 1913, pastored five churches, was interim pastor of 15 churches and retired from the pulpit in 2015 at age 102. On May 21, 2019, one day after Owens death, Dianna Cagle wrote an article about this faithful herald and defender of the truth in the Biblical Recorder, the news journal of the Baptist

---

13   Lee H. McCoy, Understanding Baptist Polity, (Nashville, Convention Press, 1964, p. 85)

State Convention of North Carolina. She explained, "Owens, who was influential in the early Conservative Resurgence movement, and Home Mission Board employee Bill Powell first started rattling Southern Baptist Convention cages about 1973 when they formed the Baptist Faith and Message Fellowship and later, the Baptist Literature Board that offered Bible study materials as an alternative to those sold by the Convention's own publishing house." [endnote]

When Owens preached his last sermon at Parkwood Baptist Church on July 26, 2015, the church celebrated Owens' 80 plus years of faithfulness in ministry. Milton Hollifield, executive director-treasurer of North Carolina's BSC, said, "M.O. Owens, Jr. is one of my great heroes. I am grateful for what he has meant to us as North Carolina Baptists and to the Southern Baptist Convention. Few people have had more influence in helping move the SBC, its seminaries and the BSC back to its conservative theological roots than Owens."

During the years of my seminary education and my first pastorate I can remember going to the annual sessions of the convention in North Carolina, and when there was any evidence of liberalism making an encroachment into Baptist life, Dr. Owens could always be found at one of the microphones to express his concerns. Sometimes he expressed concern over the leftward leanings of the Baptist colleges and sometimes it was the decidedly liberal bent of the Biblical Recorder, and in particular, the editorials of Marse Grant. His deep convictions about the integrity and infallibility of the Word of God were perpetually evident. He was a spokesman for truth and righteousness in North Carolina when other voices were sinfully silent.

William A. Powell had a similar influence in the state of Georgia. I never knew Bill Powell personally, but his fingerprints were all over the conservative movement not only in Georgia, but in the whole of our Southern Baptist Zion. On October 1, 1973 he resigned his position on the staff of the Evangelism Division of the Home Mission Board to become a part of The Baptist Faith and Message Fellowship as the editor of *The Southern Baptist Journal*. In his letter to Dr. Arthur Rutledge, President of the Home Mission Board, Powell noted his unwavering allegiance to the Southern Baptist Convention, but expressed concern "about the deep inroads that liberalism is beginning to make within our great denomination." He commented, "A lack of faith in the Bible as the infallible word of God – truth without mixture of error – is being precipitated by a few teachers and writers in some strategic places within our denomination. And the ever-enlarging emphasis placed upon the old social Gospel is dulling some of the cutting edges in evangelism."

Powell continued, "*The Southern Baptist Journal* will be Southern Baptists' first national newsmagazine. It will be a middle-of-the-road new publication for Southern Baptists. It will advocate the traditional mainline Southern Baptist positions on the Bible, missions and evangelism. One of its purposes will be to discourage churches from withdrawing from our denomination and to prevent any split within our denomination. This paper will be owned by Southern Baptist churches and yet will be completely free of any denominational control. As Chauncey Daley (editor of the Western Recorder, Kentucky Baptists' news journal) recently printed out, there is a danger in managed news and stifled criticism among Baptists, because we have our own 'Watergate' also."

Powell added, "The Baptist Faith and Message Fellowship was formed to magnify the Bible as the infallible Word of God, missions as the heartbeat of our Saviour, and evangelism as the top priority of the New Testament, and to provide a convention-wide free press." [endnote]

In 2019 *The Pathway*, news journal for the Missouri Baptist Convention, published a series of articles commemorating the history of the Conservative Resurgence in honor of its 40th anniversary. In the May 14, 2019 edition of *The Pathway*, Benjamin Hawkins, associate editor of the publication, interviewed Larry Lewis, then Director of Missions for the Mid-Missouri Baptist Association. Lewis, the first or one of the first agency leaders put in place as a result of the CR, who became president of the Home Mission Board in 1987, recalled his realization in 1973 that the "Southern Baptist Convention had radically drifted in its theology." After hearing one of Southeastern Baptist Theological Seminary's professors speak at a Bible conference, Lewis surmised, "I went from believing that anything with the name "Southern Baptist" on it was as pure as an angel to believing that we were not going to survive the 20th century as a conservative denomination if that is what he (the professor) believed."

Lewis touted Bill Powell's understanding as to how conservative Baptists could take back control of her institutions and agencies. Powell, like Patterson and Pressler, understood that electing presidents who were inerrantists who were willing to appoint conservative Baptists to serve on the Committee on Committees, which then appoints the Committee on Nominations, which then appoints the trustee boards for the various SBC agencies was the way to change the Convention. He realized that the trustees determine the leadership and the theological direction of the various agencies. Because of Powell's understanding of the way to change the course of the Convention and his commitment to that task, Lewis stated to Benjamin Hawkins in the interview, "The one guy, I think, more responsible for, more influential in the Conservative Resurgence than anybody else was William E. Powell."

In addition to better known heroes of the Conservative Resurgence men like M. O. Owens and William E. Powell were instrumental in inspiring a grassroots movement that included pastors, some denominational servants, church staff members and thousands of laypersons.

When I came back to Georgia in 1990, Pastor Wayne Hamrick was giving leadership in the Baptist quest for conservativism in the convention. Hamrick, an experienced pastor of rural churches, had unquestionable organizational ability. He had Georgia Baptist Conservatives structured and systemized like Steve Jobs had his vast Apple Corporation organized, and it was running like a well-oiled machine. The beloved leader of the conservative cause in Georgia was notorious for calling his "team captains" in the late hours of the evening. When he called me, I could easily recognize his phone number and often said to my wife, "I am about to hear the "midnight cry." Hamrick was later rewarded for his hard work by being elected president of the Georgia Baptist Convention: and he also became Chairman of the Lifeway Board of Trustees. Vance Havner, a revivalist of another generation, often said, "We will not know who the great preachers (champions for the cause of inerrancy) are until we get to heaven." Wayne Hamrick was one of the great ones.

THE PROBLEM OF CENTRALIZATION

There were primarily three reasons that prompted conservative Southern Baptists to rise up and work toward a course correction in the life of the denomination, a correction that is today called the *Conservative Resurgence.* First of all, there was the problem of centralization. As early as the 1960s it was perceived by astute observers that there were some dangerous drifts in Baptist government. Lee H. McCoy, writing in the 1964 Convention Press Publication *Understanding Baptist Polity,* has a chapter that addresses some of those dangerous drifts. One of the alarming trends foreseen by McCoy was centralism, or centralization. He writes, "Baptist government is often in danger of drifting into practices which are contrary to congregational polity. (This) may occur when one or a few individuals begin to feel that only they are able to make decisions in a Baptist body . . . . . Whenever or however a drift begins it is usually imperceptible. It is always away from democracy with more powers being exercised by individuals and less by the people as a whole." [14]

In the December 7, 1961 issue of *The Baptist Standard,* E. S. James issued a warning concerning the dangerous drift of centralism. He wrote, "not long ago the masses participated in all decisions about Baptist business and endeavors. Today there is a strong trend to leave most everything to committees and boards. This is an exceedingly dangerous move. Few would believe it could ever lead to a Baptist episcopacy, or hierarchy, but few Christians in the second century would have dreamed of such a thing as the papacy. Such things don't happen overnight. They result from a long period of delegated authority.

---

14   Pressler. Op. cit., p. 251

The only assurance against them is for all the people to know all about all the work and have a voice in all of the decisions."

The Southern Baptist Convention, as the largest evangelical denomination in America, had become what might well be called a Baptist bureaucracy. Perhaps it was not intentional in the beginning, but it appeared that the moderates gradually gained control of the agencies and institutions in the 1960s and 1970s probably thinking that they represented the theology, ideology and will of grassroots Southern Baptists. I am convinced it can be said without fear of contradiction that the average American has always detested big bureaucracy in the federal government; and there were observant Southern Baptists who became suspect of centralism and bureaucracy in the state Conventions, the national Convention, as well as their agencies and institutions prior to the Conservative Resurgence.

In the 1980s, I was pastor of Colonial Heights Baptist Church in Jackson, Mississippi. The annual session of the Convention was always held at Jackson's First Baptist Church located just across the street from the administrative office building of the Mississippi Baptist Convention Board. There were those who felt like having the annual meeting only a few yards away from the MBCB ministry center always gave the denomination's leadership a homefield advantage and the opportunity to advance the objectives deemed important to them. In many cases that was admirable; but in other ways it appeared hierarchical; and in a hierarchical society there is always a split between those who delegate and those who serve.

During those days, many of the state conventions had a pastors' conference just prior to the first session of their annual meeting, but Mississippi Baptists did not. Knowing that a pastors' conference could provide the kindling wood to ignite a passion for spiritual renewal, evangelism, and the infallibility of the Bible in the Magnolia State, plans were made to introduce the idea of a pastors' conference at the 1983 annual session of the state convention. When the Time, Place, and Preacher Committee presented their proposal for the 1984 Convention, I offered an amendment to their proposal (motion) to delay the start of the annual session from early afternoon (approximately 1:30) to the evening session (approximately 6:30) so that a pastors' conference could be scheduled for the afternoon.

Dr. Earl Kelly, the Executive Director of the MBCB, rose to speak against the motion and essentially said, "I have traveled all across this state for eleven years and I think I know the hearts of our pastors better than anyone; and I can tell you that the vast majority of them have no interest in having a pastors' conference." My amendment to the motion failed, but I was not to be deterred.

In June of 1984 Zig Ziglar, a great Southern Baptist layman and one of America's greatest motivational speakers, was elected Vice President of our national convention. I asked him if he would come and speak to a group of Mississippi Baptist pastors at one of Jackson's hotel banquet facilities between the afternoon and evening sessions on the first day of our annual meeting. He joyfully agreed to come to be our speaker (and he did so at his own expense). The dining area was filled to overflowing with pastors from all across the state. It was an incredible experience.

The news of the successful banquet apparently got back to Dr. Kelly before the evening session of the convention started. That evening he sought me out of the crowd and said he had heard that the banquet was attended by hundreds of pastors. The next day he suggested that Mississippi Baptists have a pastors' conference and he also stated that he would like to see me serve as the first president. In 1985 Mississippi Baptists had their first Pastors' Conference. It was an inspiring event for the pastors and essentially provided a chink in the armor of centralization. Dr. Earl Kelly was a great Christian statesman, who made a decision to do some decentralizing for the good of the Baptist pastors in his state.

Other Baptist leaders were far more reluctant to release control of their turf and decentralize. Consequently, that reluctance and the desire of the conservatives to make changes in the convention erupted into what Dr. Roy Honeycutt, President of Southern Baptist Theological Seminary, called, "a holy war". In his sermon "To Your Tents, O Israel" preached in the Seminary's Alumni Chapel on August 28, 1984, Honeycutt attempted to rally the seminary family and the moderate faction in the SBC to prepare for battle against the "fundamentalist" insurgence. Honeycutt thundered, "Unholy forces are now at work – which if left unchecked, will destroy essential qualities of both our convention and this seminary. (They are led by the) myopic and uninformed action of independent fundamentalist – (who intend) to hijack the Southern Baptist Convention." The Southern Seminary President was simply trying to defend his turf in a war against the majority of his own denomination that owned and funded the institution entrusted to him.

Most entity leaders were adamant about stopping the conservative juggernaut that seemed to be experiencing success in the effort to hoist the banner of Biblical inerrancy. A pivotal point came in 1984 when Charles Stanley, pastor of Atlanta's First Baptist Church agreed to be nominated as SBC Convention president after a night of agonizing prayer. Many of the denominational leaders were opposed to Stanley's election. For example, Foy Valentine was the executive director of the SBC Christian Life Commission (now the Ethics and Religious Liberty Commission) and vehemently opposed to the Conservative Resurgence. Valentine took many positions that were considered liberal. He was one of the founders of the National Abortion Rights Council, opposed the death penalty, fought the religious right, and boasted about how many messengers he recruited to attend the SBC annual meeting in Kansas City in 1984. Most of the agency heads of that day were perceived to be salaried by Southern Baptists, directed agencies funded by Southern Baptists and accountable to Southern Baptists. [15]

Two Southern Baptist seminary presidents termed both premillennialism and the resolution on the ordination of women, passed by 58 percent of the Kansas City Convention messengers, as heresy. That resolution specified, "The Scriptures teach that women are not in public worship to assume a role of authority over men lest confusion reign in the local church (I Cor. 14:33-36); and ... that we remind ourselves of the dearly bought Baptist principle of the final authority of Scripture in matters of faith and conduct and that we encourage the service of women in all aspects of church life and work other than pastoral functions and leadership roles entailing ordination." [16] The same two presidents who called that resolution heresy, called those who believed in the inerrancy of the Scripture "first century Judaizers."

In referring to this, David Simpson, editor of *The Indiana Baptist*, wrote, "The introduction of these words into the argument is an atrocity of the highest, or should I say lowest, order. Calling a person a 'heretic' in such a serious and scholarly setting is almost beyond belief. These terms clearly show that the presidents have a particular theological agenda to which they are committed. The presidents have utilized their positions of prestige and platforms for platitudes to further divide Southern Baptists." The examples of the divide are too numerous to publish or contemplate, but the "holy war" was on and the rift in the denomination was wide.

THE PROBLEM OF ACCOUNTABILITY

In the November 8, 1984, edition of the Mississippi Baptist Record, Editor Don McGregor made the following observation, "A few of Mississippi's Southern Baptists will assemble in Jackson next week to take care of the business matters for all of us. We will be few in number, for all of Mississippi's 650,000 Baptists will be represented by just a few more than two-tenths of one percent. At the bare minimum we could have 4,000 messengers registered if each church sent at least two, which is possible. Instead, there will be less than 1,500. We are used to that sort of attendance, however, and are quite comfortable with it." Historically, most state conventions have a very small minority of their constituents present for their annual meetings.

The same was also true in the national convention in the 1970s-1980s. Although the SBC annual meeting has been called one of the largest deliberative bodies in the world, only about one-hundredth of one percent attended those meetings. Furthermore, it appeared that questions calling for accountability were often summarily dismissed, called out of order, referred to some committee or tabled. Comments questioning the *Message of Genesis* by Ralph Elliott, the Baptist Joint Committee on Public Affairs, the left-leaning publications of the Sunday School Board or the liberal trend at certain seminaries appeared to be unwelcomed. Billy and Betty Baptist had little opportunity to ask for accountability under the leadership of the moderate regime.

Favoritism often contributes to the lack of accountability in Southern Baptist life. Favoritism is the practice of giving unfair preferential treatment of one person or group at the expense of another. There is a natural inclination to select individuals to be on your team who share your philosophy, interests and vision for the work you are assigned to do. This inevitably happens whether moderates or conservatives, Democrats or Republicans, capitalists or socialists are in control. Trustees who are supposed to represent the Baptists in the pew often become ingratiated by an agency leader, enamored by the position itself, and captivated by the amenities offered to those who hold that strategic role. Consequently, the attraction to rubber stamp the agenda and wishes of the entity leader can easily take precedence over the need to make the administration accountable. However, being a trustee of a Baptist entity is far more than an honor to be coveted, it is a serious and solemn responsibility to be upheld.

I was a trustee on the Baptist Sunday School Board during Lloyd Elder's tenure as president. He was a gracious and personable Christian gentleman who appeared to be a centrist in terms of his leadership and theology – an admitted inerrantist. However, as the controversy heightened, Elder became more combative and clearly identified with the moderate Baptist effort to maintain control of the denomination. Although Elder became president of the Sunday School Board in 1983, his first major trial came in 1985 when protest erupted over a Sunday School lesson in which the Satan of Job 1 and 2 was described as "a kind of heavenly inspector" for sin, "and God's servant, not His enemy," but not "the devil of the New Testament". [17] Other challenges were to follow. President Elder was asked to apologize for publishing a message his predecessor, James Sullivan gave in the agency's chapel service in which he compared "ultra-conservatives" in the convention to "Pharisaical legalists, extreme literalists, and snake handlers." The motion by conservative trustees that requested an apology from Elder failed by a 33-40 vote. [18]

The President of the BSSB joined Russell Dilday, President of Southwestern Baptist Theological Seminary, and Keith Parks, President of The Foreign Mission Board, in opposing the defunding of the Baptist Joint Committee on Public Affairs, an entity that had long failed to represent grassroots Southern Baptists with its liberal position on issues like religious freedom and sanctity of life. Even though other matters of concern to the conservative trustees arose frequently, Dr. Elder's leadership was endorsed by a majority of trustees who appeared to be more interested in showing deference to the president than being accountable to the Baptists in the pew who by a vast majority always maintained an uncompromising allegiance to the Word of God.

In the corporate world, trustees protect the best interests of their shareholders. They want the company to grow and prosper, but at the end of the day they are responsible for providing a good return on the investment of those who own stock in the company. In the denominational world those shareholders are the tithers who purchase an interest (shares) in the ministries of the Convention through deposits in the

---

17   Ibid, p. 107

18   Ibid, p. 110

offering plate. Good trustees will also make wise, Christ-honoring decisions when choosing entity leaders, be wary of nepotism, and avoid things that would suggest a conflict of interest. Any leader of a Baptist agency should be a sold-out Christian with a clear biblical worldview, have a passion for Christ, be a personal soul-winner, and completely committed to the purpose of the entity.

Furthermore, trustees should make sure that the entity leader is building a team of workers that are marked by an explicit agreement, a visible unity, extraordinary prayer, high motivation, and a high level of collaboration with constituents and/or partners to work efficiently and effectively to fulfill the Great Commission. If our agencies are not committed to these things it is unlikely that their employees will rise above the example of their leaders.

THE PROBLEM OF LIBERALISM

The scope of liberalism in Southern Baptist institutions and agencies prior to the Conservative Resurgence was widespread and damaging. Many of the details of the convention's theological drift have been highlighted in books written and published previous to this tome. It is not the purpose of this book to restate the extent of that liberalism. However, I have seen what happens when aspiring young ministerial students go off to school to prepare for the calling which God has placed upon their lives and they are taught spurious and errant theology and exposed to values that are not consistent with God's Word.

In the midst of the Conservative Resurgence a friend gave me a book entitled *The Long Way Home* by John P. Jewell Jr. The book perfectly illustrates the dilemma caused by a liberal theological education. Jewell went to William Jewell Baptist College in Liberty, Missouri with a burning desire to preach the message of Jesus Christ. He recalled, "A passion was kindled within my being to tell the story of Jesus Christ. The passion burned so, I thought it must have been what Cleopas and his traveling companion on the Emmaus Road felt, ..."Did not our heart burn within us. . .?" (Luke 24:32).

Jewell continued, "When I entered William Jewell, I was committed to the idea that the Scriptures were inspired by God and that they were absolutely authoritative for the life of the church and the life of the saints. It was a part of my spiritual inheritance. I had personally experienced the power of the Scriptures to call me to new life and growth. . . .My acceptance of the Scriptures as inspired by God was one of the cornerstones in my faith in Christ and ministry to His church." [19]

However, when Jewell began to be exposed to the teachings of the religion professors at his chosen college, he indicated that he felt like they were trying to pry him loose from what they called "his terribly archaic view of the Word of God." He explained, "Each night was a wrestling match! What was I going to accept and what was I going to reject? . . .I was beginning. . . . to get the strong impression that some of the faculty carried a big theological chip on their shoulder. You could boil all the ethereal and sophisticated jargon we were hearing down to a fairly simple statement, 'Smart people don't believe the Bible!" Jewell became so disillusioned that he began to think about abandoning his calling and education and get a job as a truck driver or carpenter – jobs that

---

19   Ibid., p. 58

would keep him from having to evaluate every new idea that came along. [20]

Looking back on his college experience Jewell recalled, "Over the past twenty years as I have lived the pain of the loss of faith and talked with so many others who have traveled the same path, I've seen this one common theme emerge almost without fail. The inexorable slide toward a loss of faith began with a surrender of the view that the Scriptures were inspired. Sometimes it was wholesale tossing off of the inspiration of the Bible. Most times, however, it was an inch-by-inch surrender. A kind of a 'Yes, but . . "approach to the question, "Hath God said?" Jewell repeatedly heard, "The Bible is not the Word of God, but rather the words of God. The Bible contains the word of God." [21] Such an interpretation of the Bible's worth is disingenuous if not damaging.

Jewell warned, "The rejection of the Bible as the Word of God has somehow come to be assumed as a requisite of intelligent, thinking people. Be sure and be warned! Once you begin that surrender, however slight you may think it is, you have engaged in a process that does not end until every major foundation for faith and ministry has been destroyed. I have scores of friends who will argue that they have discovered new foundations and a new kind of faith, but with rare exceptions their churches are not ruled by Christ, and there is no desire to reach people with the Gospel." [22]

John Jewell, Jr. started his theological education with a firm faith, a burning passion to preach, high hopes for a successful ministry, but fifteen years later his marriage was as fragile as a feather in a windstorm, his son had become a

---

20   Ibid. p. 59

21   Ibid. p. 84-85

22   Ibid p. 85

prodigal living in San Francisco, and he was battling serious emotional trauma. He summarized his perilous journey thusly, "I spent years wandering in a hopeless maze of theological confusion, shallow fads and personal turmoil." [23]

Jewell finally extricated himself from his quagmire of confusion and apostasy and after many dangers, toils and snares made his way back from his long journey into the far country and enjoyed a fruitful and fulfilling ministry. Unfortunately, many others did not. Consequently, there was a cry from grassroots Baptists for a renewed emphasis on the infallibility of the Word of God and a resurgence.

---

23   Ibid p 10

CHAPTER 2

A VICTORY WORTHY OF NOTICE TO A WATCHING WORLD

THE CONSERVATIVE RESURGENCE DID NOT PROVOKE any physical battles to my knowledge. There were no rocket launchers or assault weapons employed, nor did I hear of anyone resorting to fisticuffs or pugilistic encounters, for that matter. The "holy war" was more of a battle of principles, polities, philosophies and theologies. However, it was a mighty confrontation that resulted in a series of great victories for those who had an uncompromising allegiance to the fidelity and reliability of God's infallible Word. Many stated that no Christian denomination or body had ever reclaimed the fundamentals of the faith once they had been distorted or twisted by those with a liberal bent. We can rightly conclude that the Conservative Resurgence was a miracle – a phenomenon of gargantuan proportions.

GIDEON AND HIS BAND OF MEN

The Bible narrative that immediately comes to mind when I think of the battle for the Bible in the second half of the 20th century in Southern Baptist life is the confrontation between Gideon and his 300 valiant men and the mighty army of Midian in the valley near the hill of Moreh. Gideon considered himself unworthy of being anyone's champion. When God called him to lead the Israelites into battle against the Midianites Gideon declared, "O my Lord, how can I save Israel? Indeed my clan is the weakest in Manasseh, and I am the least in my father's house." (Judges 6:15). Common sense would lead one to believe that "poor" and "least" do not necessarily make a good combination for victory.

Some scholars contend that Manasseh was the least significant of the twelve tribes, sometimes even referred to as a half-tribe. Furthermore, Gideon claimed that his family was among the poorest of clans in the weakest tribe and that he was the most unlikely person in his family to do anything of significance. A careful study of the Bible would indicate that some of Gideon's protests were probably more indicative of an excuse than a substantial reason, but the truth is that his resume was not obviously impressive.

And yet God used Gideon in a miraculous way to overcome the intimidating Midianite army. With only 300 soldiers he routed the enemy that vastly outnumbered his band of faithful men. Interestingly, when they broke their pitchers to let their lights shine and blew their trumpets, their battle cry was "the sword of the Lord and Gideon." The sword of the Lord, the Word of God is always "quick and powerful and sharper than any two-edged sword." (Hebrews 4:12). Gideon and his faithful men won the victory against overwhelming odds.

While the Conservative Resurgence was designed by men of courage and wisdom and while they were supported by great men who pastored some of the nation's most influential churches they were facing monumental opposition - a well-established denominational structure, strong leaders solidly entrenched in historic institutions, notable pastors in strategic churches, and a Baptist Press and many state Baptist publications that were protective and supportive of the establishment in spite of the liberal drift of the Convention.

THE SIX DAY WAR IN 1967

In reflecting on the fundamentalist victory in Southern Baptist life I also began to think of some of the notable victories of my lifetime. One of the most notable was the dramatic victory of Israel in what has come to be called the Six Day War, which took place in June of 1967. The combined allied Arab forces of Egypt, Syria, Jordan and Iraq, with nearly half a million troops, were set to virtually annihilate Israel, whose military force was barely half of the Arab forces. In addition, those Arab forces were backed by the Soviet Union, an undeniable world superpower.

The Arabs had four aircraft for every one military plane possessed by Israel, and twice the number of tanks.

Israel appealed to the United States for help, but our country refused to support the Israelis for fear of Russian retaliation. The situation was tense as the allied nations positioned themselves for the invasion of the Holy Land. Syria was already launching rockets from their strategic vantage point on the Golan Heights. The Egyptians would not let Israel's ships through the Straits of Tiran. The president of Iraq vowed that his country's goal was to "wipe Israel off the map." [24]

The Israelis spoke of a massive slaughter and prepared for what they feared would be a second Holocaust. D. Thomas Lancaster, writing about the miraculous deliverance of Israel from her enemies, states,

> *By June 5, the outbreak of hostilities seemed inevitable. Five Egyptian divisions of ground troops and two divisions of armor occupied the Sinai, ready to roll into Israel. Hundreds of tanks stood ready opposite Eilat, prepared to topple the Negev. The Jordanian army had placed thousands of soldiers and hundreds of tanks on the West Bank and along Israel's eastern border. Reinforcements from Iraq stood ready. On the northern border, Syrian soldiers on the Golan Heights dug in for a long fight.*
>
> *"Before the Arab nations could strike, Israel launched preemptive airstrikes against Egyptian airfields. As the Israeli Air Force took to the sky, the first miracle of the war occurred. Jordanian radar detected the planes and tried to warn Egypt, but the Egyptians had changed their coding frequencies the previous day and had not yet updated the Jordanians with the new codes. The message never went through, giving Israel the element*

---

24 https://ffoz.org/discover/messiah-magazine/miracles-of-the-six-day-war.html/Accessed March 23, 2021

of surprise. The Egyptians had no time to react. "The Israeli Air Force destroyed six Egyptian airfields and hundreds of Egyptians planes. In a single day, Israel destroyed the Egyptian and Syrian Air Forces. The Egyptian Air Force never even had a chance to leave the ground. That same day, the Israelis launched a ground offensive into the Gaza Strip and the Sinai, catching Egyptian troops completely by surprise. Israeli tanks and ground forces rolled into the heavily defended Sinai and quickly punched a hole through the lines. They advanced so rapidly that, again, the Egyptian forces scarcely had time to react."[25]

I am not using the Six Day War to illustrate the intensity or the fierceness of the battle to win back the conservative standard which had once dominated the Southern Baptist landscape, but I mention it because the victory was nothing short of miraculous. However, to be honest, there were those in the battle for the Bible in the SBC who were scarred much deeper than if they had been shredded by shrapnel – some on both sides of the campaign.

NO JOY IN MUDVILLE

The Conservative movement was carefully crafted by knowledgeable architects who developed a proposal that was thoughtfully conceived and designed with understanding. To most active Southern Baptists, the names of Paige Patterson and Paul Pressler have been attached to the conservative fight for the inerrancy of the Bible in Southern Baptist life. Howev-

---

25   Ibid., p. 3

er, it became a grassroots movement that included thousands of pastors, a smattering of denominational leaders, many church staff, and a countless number of laypersons.

The election of Adrian Rogers, pastor of Bellevue Baptist Church in Memphis, TN, to the presidency at the Houston Convention in 1979 was the first major victory for the conservative contingent of Southern Baptists. Thomas S. Kidd and Barry Hankins stated, "The election of Adrian Rogers set in motion a political and theological battle for control of America's largest Protestant denomination. It would become one of the most significant religious events of the twentieth century." [26]

Although Dr. Rogers was opposed by five worthy candidates, he won on the first ballot by receiving 6,129 of the votes, representing 51.36 percent of the ballots cast. There was great joy in Houston when the results of the election were announced. Although Dr. Rogers was extremely popular, it took no small effort to win the victory. And though it was just the first round in the battle for Biblical fidelity in the Southern Baptist Convention, those who supported Rogers for president celebrated the election win, believing that it was the beginning of a new era in the denomination. It was a significant victory, but there would be more to come.

The moderates were obviously despondent and disappointed over the outcome of the election. In *Love Worth Finding*, the biography of Adrian Rogers, written by his wife, Joyce, she made the following comment about the outcome of the election: "There was joy on the faces of many and bewilderment on the faces of others."

At the time of the announcement of the winner of the election, I was seated near Bill Self, an Atlanta pastor, who

---

26 Thomas S. Kidd and Barry Hankins, *Baptists in America: A History* (Oxford University Press, Oxford, England, 2015) p. 228

came in third place in the vote for president with 1,673 votes. It was obvious that he was not overcome with joy. In fact, I noticed that the countenances of many moderates appeared to be marked by gloom, despair and agony. They knew they were in a battle for the heart and soul of the denomination and the first round had not gone well for them.

I had friends in the moderate camp. They were good people – some were denominational loyalists who could not see any reason for the conflict. Others identified with the moderate camp not because of their theology, but because of their friendships with those opposed to the conservative uprising. Then, of course, there were those who were absolutely committed to the liberal theology that had ignited the ire of those who wanted to turn the Convention back to its theological moorings. However, all of those who had voted for moderate candidates were greatly perplexed.

And for some strange reason I was reminded of Ernest Lawrence Thayer's poem, "Casey at the Bat." The Mudville baseball team was losing the game 4-2 in the last inning. The hope of winning the game for the Mudville faithful was slipping away. The first two batters made outs, but then Flynn singled and Blake doubled, which gave mighty Casey another opportunity to bat.

Thayer pens the last segment of the famed poem:

"On somewhere in this favored land the sun is shining bright,
The band is playing somewhere and somewhere hearts are light,
And somewhere men are laughing, and somewhere children shout,
But there is no joy in Mudville – mighty Casey has struck out."[27]

---

27   https://poets.org/poem/casey-bat/Accessed March 23, 2021

ADRIAN ROGERS - A SPIRITUAL GIANT

The disappointment of almost 50 percent of the Convention messengers was painfully obvious, but there were also shouts of conquest in Houston after the winner of the presidential race was announced. Our children were particularly happy about the election of Adrian Rogers. Our identical twin sons were always captivated by his ability to tell them apart. They didn't see him but once a year - at the annual session of the convention, but he would greet them, stand back, and say, "This one is John and this one is Jerry." It may have just been lucky guesses, but his ability to identify them was more than their grandmother could do on many occasions.

Dr. Rogers was always personable and was known for his commanding presence, charisma, mellifluous voice, and authoritative demeanor. He was a logical thinker, a man of wisdom, and a powerful preacher. When he entered a room all the others generally deferred to his leadership. The new convention president set the wheels in motion for the Conservative Resurgence by following the prescribed plan of appointing staunch inerrantists to the Committee on Committees, the group responsible for nominating the Committee on Nominations, who in turn would nominate the Board of Trustees for the various institutions and agencies. A strict adherence to the appointing of conservative people to the Committee on Committees could, within three or four years, alter the theological trajectory of the denomination.

The victory was not easily won, and came with many dangers, toils and snares. After his first year in office, Dr. Rogers opted not to run for what traditionally had been an obligatory second term for former presidents. He knew that if he were elected to another one-year term at the St. Louis Convention in 1980, a new president would have to be elected at the 1981 Convention in Los Angeles and that it might be difficult to get a conservative candidate elected so far away from the Bible Belt. His decision was also due in part to having had gall bladder surgery and the need to recover from that. When Rogers addressed the convention messengers in St. Louis in 1980 to explain his reason for not being a presidential candidate for another term, he explained, "Being the president of the Southern Baptist Convention has made this an interesting year. But I want you to know that I have slept like a baby almost every night for the past year. I woke up every two hours and cried." Being president of the country's largest non-Catholic denomination can be taxing and demanding under normal circumstances, but to serve as president in the midst of a huge controversy can take an exacting toll on the hardiest of souls.

THE GOOD NEWS AND BAD NEWS

When it became obvious that Dr. Rogers had chosen not to serve a second term as president, he called Dr. Bailey Smith, pastor of First Southern Baptist Church in Del City, Oklahoma, and said, "I have talked to the men that we think are our leaders, and they want you to be nominated. Will you do it?" The Oklahoma pastor responded in the affirmative; and explained, "Adrian's response was typical of his creative mind. He said, 'Well, the good news is that you will probably win. The bad news is you will probably win.'" [28]

---

28   Smith, Bailey, A Life Without Compromise: The Life and Ministry of Bailey Smith (January 2019), p. 106.

The Del City pastor was elected on the first ballot with 51.67 percent of the vote over five other candidates. At age 41, he became the youngest person ever to be elected as president of the Southern Baptist Convention. The phenomenal evangelistic spirit in his church and his growing reputation as a dynamic preacher had won him favor with conservatives from California to Virginia. *Time Magazine* described him as "a formidable figure, a fiery, red-haired, old-style prairie stem winder." *Christianity Today* called him "an inerrancy superstar."

Smith, never known for mincing words, incurred the wrath of many Baptist state paper editors and others who did not like his straightforward, seemingly unvarnished comments. For example, in the summer of 1980 Smith spoke at a Public Affairs briefing in Dallas where he made his much-heralded statement, "God does not hear the prayers of the Jews." Thirty-eight years later I personally asked Bailey if he was still committed to that statement. He said, "Absolutely! The Bible says, 'For there is one God and one Mediator between God and men, the man Christ Jesus'" (I Timothy 2:5). The Convention president was castigated by the secular press and many Baptist publications for his comment, but here is the rest of the story: following his comment about the Jews, President Smith met with Jewish leadership and the relationship between Jews and Christians was actually strengthened. [29]

Smith was re-elected to a second term at the Los Angeles Convention in 1981, garnering 60.24 percent of the votes over Baylor University President Dr. Abner McCall. He continued to appoint solid conservatives to the Committee on Committees and by the completion of his second term the tide was beginning to turn in favor of an inerrancy resurgence. As the

---

29   Pressler, Paul, A Hill on Which to Die, One Southern Baptist's Journey, (Broadman & Holman Publishers, Nashville, TN. 1999) p. 118.

winning streak continued, the number of people identifying with the conservative cause increased and the victory celebrations were marked with greater enthusiasm.

JIMMY DRAPER ELECTED PRESIDENT

More then 20,000 messengers flocked to New Orleans in June of 1982 for the annual meeting of the Southern Baptist Convention and elected another conservative, Dr. Jimmy Draper, pastor of First Baptist Church of Euless, Texas. He was elected on the second ballot by a 56.97 percent margin over 43.03 percent for Dr. Duke McCall, who had recently retired as president of Southern Seminary, and who was succeeded by Dr. Roy L. Honeycutt. At this 1982 convention, resolutions were approved endorsing scientific creationism, sanctioning an amendment regarding voluntary prayer in public schools, and supporting a constitutional amendment prohibiting abortion. These were resolutions that represented a distinctively conservative, Biblical worldview commensurate with the vast majority of Southern Baptists.

Draper, an effective pastor and capable leader who was widely known for being a congenial and generous Christian gentleman, was re-elected unopposed for a second term at the 1983 Convention in Pittsburgh. That Draper was unopposed was not surprising to me. Let me illustrate: a couple from Draper's church in Euless moved from Texas to Jackson, Mississippi and began attending the church where I served as pastor and told me about their first visit to First Baptist Church in Euless. They went to the later Sunday morning service in Euless and when they left the church to go home, their car would not start. When Draper had con-cluded shaking hands with the worshippers as they exited the church, he saw the dilemma of this couple and walked over to their car to offer assistance. When they explained that their car would not start. The Euless pastor said, "My wife and I each drove our cars to church this morning, so you take my car and use it today and when you come back to the evening service, I will see that your car is running and ready for you to drive home". When the couple returned that evening their car was fitted with a new battery and ready to be driven.

Draper continued the principle of appointing conser-vatives to the Committee on Committees; and the balance of power was shifting significantly. It was in Pittsburgh that Charles Stanley, pastor of First Baptist Church in Atlanta, Georgia became visible on the national convention platform. He was president of the Pastors' Conference and the chairman of the Committee on Boards (Nominations), much to the ire of the liberals/moderates who had tried to exclude him from any involvement in Southern Baptist life. His growing InTouch television ministry had earned him the title of "America's Pas-tor," and they knew that his popularity across the nation was enormous, and that he was a staunch conservative.

THE MODERATES NEMESIS - CHARLES STANLEY

The moderates, realizing that the Southern Baptist Pastors' Conference preceding the annual sessions of the Convention each year provided a rallying cry for conserva-tives, decided to provide an alternative conference in 1984, called the SBC Forum. The speakers included Ken Chafin, pastor of South Main Baptist Church in Houston, TX, Duke McCall, former President of Southern Baptist Theological Seminary in Louisville, Kirby Godsey, President of Mercer University and David Matthews, Pastor of First Baptist Church in Greenville, SC. It appeared to be one last convulsive effort to prevent the Conservatives from returning the denomination to its Biblical roots.

When the messengers gathered in Kansas City for the 1984 Convention, there was no specific candidate that had been announced for the presidency for the conservatives. On the night prior to the election a prayer vigil had failed to provide clarity as to who should be nominated. It was not until mid-morning on the day of the election that Charles Stanley indicated to a select group of prayer partners that he felt that God had given him the freedom to have his name placed before the messengers as a candidate for president. He was elected on the first ballot with 52.18 percent (7,692) of the votes over moderate Grady Cothen with 26.28 percent of the votes and independent John Sullivan with 21.53 percent of the votes.

In Kansas City, a resolution "On the Ordination and Role of Women in Ministry" was adopted by more than 58 percent of the messengers, stating,

"WHEREAS, the Scriptures teach that women are not in public worship to assume a role of authority over men lest confusion reign in the local church (I Corinthians 14:33-36); and

WHEREAS, while Paul commends women and men alike in other roles of ministry and service (Titus 2:1-10) he excludes women from pastoral leadership (I Timothy 2:12) to preserve a submission God requires be-

cause the man was the first in creation and the woman was first in the Edenic fall (I Timothy 2:13ff)."

The vote provided clear evidence that the tide was turning in favor of the fundamentalist camp.

Following Stanley's election, several denominational executives launched an all-out attack designed to make sure he did not win a second term as President of the SBC at the 1985 Convention in Dallas. The momentum began to build, and for a full year every indication was that Southern Baptists were headed for something akin to the so-called Rumble in the Jungle in 1974 when George Foreman, the undefeated world heavyweight champion faced challenger Muhammad Ali, the former heavyweight champion, in Kinshasa, Zaire (now Democratic Republic of the Congo).

The 1985 Southern Baptist Convention meeting in Dallas was historic. Baptist Press declared, "By some estimates, the 45,519 registered messengers may have constituted the largest deliberative body ever assembled." Gregory Willis, professor of church history and dean of Southern Baptist Theological Seminary's school of theology called it "a watershed moment in the conservative revolution in the convention." Moderate leader Cecil Sherman declared that it was the first time he contemplated losing the battle for the SBC.

The massive convention center in Dallas opened its doors at 600 A.M. and long lines formed earlier than that in order for messengers to claim seats for the representatives from their churches. Bill Davidson, the Minister of Education for our church in Jackson, got to the Dallas Convention Center and staked out a claim for fifteen seats for the messengers from our church and we remained in those seats from early morning until the Benediction was pronounced at the end of the evening session. We sent two of our messengers to purchase food for us after the morning session and again prior to the evening session. We dared not leave our seats for fear of losing them to some beloved interlopers.

David Roach, writing for Baptist Press 30 years after the much-heralded convention, explained,

"For pastor's wife Ritchie Hale, attending the 1985 Southern Baptist Convention annual meeting meant sleeping in a 1960 popup camper with her husband and four children amid 100-degree temperatures and thunderstorms. Hale, whose husband Sheldon pastored Liberty Baptist Church in Auburn, Ky., at the time, was willing to endure the steamy popup camper parked some 30 miles from the convention center and dressing four children in their Sunday clothes in campground bathhouses, because she believed reelecting the conservative Charles Stanley as SBC president could make an eternal difference." [30]

Pastors from small rural churches drove through the night in order to vote for Charles Stanley for president. Others, who longed to see the convention embrace the cause of Biblical infallibility, came and slept in their cars or tents, because they could not afford a hotel room. Others packed food for the several days they were going to be in Dallas, because they could not afford to eat in restaurants.

Commenting on this convention, Jerry Vines remarked,

---

30   https://www.baptistpress.com/resource-library/news/1985-dallas-
     -sbc-a-watershed-moment/Accessed March 23, 2021

"The convention sessions themselves were studies in chaos. People were jammed in the hall, and the room was rather hot. Tempers flared. . . A conservative pastor of mine got into a nose to nose with a moderate pastor. 'We need someone to pray,' someone suggested. They called upon me. Hardly neutral, I prayed as best and as quickly as I could. A bad scene was averted." [31]

In the midst of the most memorable convention in my recollection, Charles Stanley was elected by winning 55.3 percent or 24,453 votes over Amarillo, Texas, Pastor Winford Moore's 44.7 percent.

Following the 1985 convention Robert and Julia Crowder brought a lawsuit against the Southern Baptist Convention because they did not like one of Charles Stanley's rulings at the annual session in Dallas. The lawsuit was decided in favor of the convention, but Stanley did not want the convention to experience anything like that again, so he secured the services of one of America's premier parliamentarians, Dr. Barry McCarty, who has been serving in that role to the present.

THE PEACE COMMITTEE

Stanley appointed a 22-member Peace Committee to study the causes of the controversy and recommend possible solutions. Perhaps the most memorable comment and defining moment in the entire Conservative Resurgence was when

---

31 Vines, Jerry. Vines, My Life and Ministry, (B&H Publishing Group, Nashville, Tennessee, 2014), p. 143

Adrian Rogers offered a memorable statement about his position on the Word of God to the Peace Committee. It is a statement that will be etched in Southern Baptist history until Jesus comes. Someone asked him why everyone could not just get together. He said,

"I'm willing to compromise about many things, but not the Word of God. So far as getting together is concerned, we don't have to get together. The Southern Baptist Convention, as it is, does not have to survive. I don't have to be the pastor of Bellevue Baptist Church. I don't have to be loved; I don't even have to live. But I will not compromise the Word of God." [32]

Walter Shurden, moderate church historian, who as dean of Southern Seminary's school of theology in the early 1980s, viewed Rogers as the crucial figure in the SBC's conservative movement. He explained,

"I sincerely doubt ... that fundamentalism could have known its measure of success apart from Adrian Rogers. No other fundamentalist could rival him as preacher, debater, or intransigent believer. When the leadership of the fundamentalists met for their strategy sessions, the press releases often read, 'Adrian Rogers presided.' He was by far fundamentalists' most capable leader and moderates' most formidable opponent." [33]

---

32   Adrian Rogers: 32 Years in Camelot, The Christian Index, August 16, 2017.

33   https://www.baptistpress.com/resource-library/news/adrian-rogers-
     -rising-star-of-memphis-elected-35-years-ago/Accessed March 23, 2021

Dr. Rogers was elected president again in 1986 and 1987, and by the time he had finished his third term, the influence of the Conservative Resurgence was being felt in most facets of Southern Baptists life. Recently elected entity trustees were fulfilling their fiduciary duties as they dealt with issues long neglected by those who had preceded them. Strong conservatives were placed in strategic leadership roles. Larry L. Lewis was elected as president of the Home Mission Board, Lewis Drummond elected president of Southeastern Seminary, and Richard Land elected head of the SBC Christian Life Commission by fundamentalist trustees. Resolutions reflecting uncompromising biblical principles were being passed; and messengers were returning home from the annual convention meetings with the full assurance that significant battles were being won and that victory was on the horizon.

Southern Baptists continued to elect presidents with an uncompromising allegiance to the Word of God. The margins of victory for the conservative presidential candidates were increasing significantly and the convention was returning to its theological moorings. The Pastors' Conference at First Baptist Church in Jacksonville started relatively small in 1985, but after the construction of the new worship center, the conference began attracting thousands of pastors and laity every January. Each meeting was marked by a revival-like atmosphere and fueled the fires for the Conservative Resurgence in Southern Baptist life. The church's co-pastors, Homer Lindsay, Jr and Jerry Vines, became champions for the cause, particularly among grassroots, rural, small-church pastors.

The 1988 Convention was held in San Antonio, Texas, and presided over by President Adrian Rogers. There are three things that stand out in my mind about that particular convention: First, there was a heated debate over Resolution #5 on The Priesthood of the Believer. Moderates made motions and amendments accusing the Resolution Committee of elevating the pastor to a position of "papal authority" in the church and infringing upon the "soul competency" of believers. The resolution passed by a percentage vote of 54.75 to 45.25, but not without considerable examination, deliberation and argumentation.

Second, there was the victory of Jerry Vines, who won the presidency on the first ballot over a formidable opponent, Arizona Pastor Dr. Richard Jackson, of the North Phoenix Baptist Church, who was conservative in his theology, but somehow had chosen to identify with the moderate faction of the denomination.

The third thing that stands out about the San Antonio convention was what Judge Pressler called "a sophomoric, melodramatic gesture" on the part of Randall Lolley, president of Southeastern Baptist Theological Seminary, who made a grand exodus from the convention hall and led a small contingent of allies to the Alamo several blocks away to ceremoniously burn their ballots. [34] Lolley was defiantly protesting Vines' election and what he perceived to be the sure advancing of the conservative juggernaut.

The presidency of Jerry Vines was characterized by an emphasis on soul winning. First Baptist Church in Jacksonville was a great soul winning church and soon after his election Vines announced that soul winning would be the theme of his presidency. He explained,

"I recommitted myself to being a faithful witness for the Lord. I purchased a little red notebook and recorded the date, name, and some brief explanation about the people I won to the Lord that year. I was not doing this

---

34 Pressler, op. cit. p. 141

*to be a show-off. I was trying to set an example for our
Southern Baptist leaders and people.*"[35]

I distinctly remember Jerry Vines preaching a sermon on personal witnessing at the convention a year later, holding up that little red book and rejoicing that the Lord had given him the grace and joy of leading 52 individuals to Christ that first year of his presidency, the last one being on staff of the Hilton Hotel where he was staying in Las Vegas for the convention.

Throughout the 20ᵗʰ Century Southern Baptists continued to elect presidents committed to the veracity and fidelity of Holy Scripture including Morris Chapman, Edwin Young, Jim Henry, Tom Elliff and Paige Patterson. Elliff and Patterson were the first two presidents to be elected unopposed in the first year they were nominated during the entire Conservative Resurgence indicating that the battle had been won. The divide between the conservatives and moderates became more definitive as moderates began to formulate their own seminaries, their own news journal, and their own alternative pseudo-denomination (the Cooperative Baptist Fellowship).

In 1998 Paige Patterson was elected president at the Convention in Salt Lake City, Utah. In that annual session Southern Baptist messengers approved a motion calling for the appointment of a committee to study its Baptist Faith and Message statement and bring a report to the 2000 convention meeting in Orlando, Florida. T. C. Pinkney, the editor of the Baptist Banner, a Virginia-based conservative journal, made the motion, stating,

---

35   Vines, op. cit. p. 165

"The intervening 36 years have been momentous ones for the Southern Baptist Convention. I believe it is appropriate at this time that the Baptist Faith and Message be reviewed and that it be made consistent with the current stand of the Southern Baptist Convention."

The motion was approved by a 54-46 percent vote. [36]

At the Orlando Convention the messengers overwhelmingly adopted the revised Baptist Faith and Message 2000. Julian Motley, writing for Baptist Press, stated,

"For twenty years, Southern Baptist Convention messengers have been backing away from the influence of neo-orthodoxy. In Orlando they finally backed all the way out the door and shut it. This middle of the road neo-orthodox theology, with its low view of Scripture, had become increasingly entrenched in our colleges and seminaries since the early part of the twentieth century. Not all messengers at the Orlando Convention may have fully understood all that the revisions meant, but a decisive break with the influence of neo-orthodoxy is certainly what was intended and is clearly what the messengers pray was accomplished." [37]

In the biography of her husband, Adrian Rogers, Joyce Rogers wrote,

---

36   https://www.baptistpress.com/resource-library/news/messengers-a-gree-to-study-baptist-faith-and-message/Accessed March 23, 2021

37   https://www.baptistpress.com/resource-library/sbc-life-articles/what-southern-baptists-really-did-in-orlando/Accessed March 23, 2021

"Conservative presidents continued to be elected, and the boards and agencies began to be filled with those who took a strong stand for the inerrancy of the Bible. The unthinkable had happened. The dictum of history is that institutions and organizations that move to the left never turn around. Usually new entities must be raised up to stand for conservative causes. But now the gigantic Southern Baptist Convention had turned back to its roots and its once-solid biblical stance." [38]

Jerry Vines added in his autobiography,

"The 'impossible' was occurring. A denomination was being turned from liberalism back to conservatism." [39]

For a number of years many of us had languished under the teaching of those who embraced the theology of neo-orthodoxy. We felt like the Israelites who had been taken into captivity by the Babylonians. Psalm 137 describes the pathetic, plaintive, sorrowful plight of God's people when they wept in a foreign land and could not sing the songs of Zion. They hung their harps on the willow trees beside the river, because they had no use for these instruments of joy. Like the Israelites we wondered if there was any possibility of our joy being restored, if there could be a time when we could take our harps off the willows and sing and rejoice, because of the Word of the Lord being honored and taught with conviction and power.

---

38   Rogers, op. cit. p. 110

39   Vines, op. cit. p. 137

By the late 1980s, many of us were removing our harps from the willows. We had reason to sing the songs of Zion. We could rejoice, because the Word of the Lord was being restored to its rightful place as the 'theopnuestos' – the God-breathed, infallible truth of God.

However, I have recently wondered, was our celebration of victory premature, did we remove the harps from the willows too soon?

CHAPTER 3

THE DEVIL DECEIVES
TO DESTROY

THE ANSWER TO THE QUESTION at the end of the previous chapter is "yes!" It has become apparent over the past two decades that we did take the harps off the willow too soon, because while we can celebrate temporary victories on this earth, the ultimate celebration will have to wait until we get to heaven. We have an adversary, a formidable foe. He is walking about like a roaring lion seeking to do his malicious work. He seems to be more active and intent on creating chaos than ever. His attacks seem to be more frequent and forceful than ever.

Let us consider how Satan strategizes to defeat the people of God and the church which He bought with His blood. If Satan cannot accomplish his diabolical scheme through an open confrontation, he will do it through his old standby *modus operandi* of subtilty and deceit. He tries to accomplish his purposes through those who are devoted to his objectives, but when that fails he will attempt to influence blood-bought believers to do his bidding. If Lucifer finds a chink in the armor of a born-again Christian, he will exploit it; and if he discovers that a church is weak or susceptible in one specific area, he will devise, with great craftiness, a plan to wreak havoc in that church.

When Southern Baptists became secure in their glorious victory in the Conservative Resurgence, the god of this world began to explore ways to once again cripple the greatest evangelistic and missionary force in the modern world.

Thomas Jefferson is attributed with the oft quoted phrase: "The price of liberty is eternal vigilance." What is true for the nation is true for the denomination as well; our freedoms are always at risk. If the virtue of eternal vigilance is abandoned, servitude is at once the consequence of that crime, and the punishment for that abandonment

The American abolitionist Wendell Phillips, in a speech he made on January 28, 1852, inverted Jefferson's statement, and exclaimed,

> *"Eternal vigilance is the price of liberty; power is ever stealing from the many to the few. The manna of popular liberty must be gathered each day, or it is rotten. The living sap of today outgrows the dead rind of yesterday. The hand entrusted with power becomes, either from human depravity or esprit de corps, the necessary enemy of the people. Only by continued oversight can the democrat in office be prevented from hardening into a despot; only by unintermitted agitation can a people*

be sufficiently awake to principle not to let liberty be smothered in material prosperity."[40]

However, eternal vigilance is needed not only for the liberty and freedom of a nation or a suppressed race of people, but for the preservation of all that is noble and good, because the devil's everlasting intent is "to steal, and to kill, and to destroy" (John 10:10). If one of Satan's disgusting plans to wreck a Christian's witness, a church's mission, or a denomination's divine enterprise is foiled, he will devise another way to ruin it.

SATAN'S EFFORT TO DESTROY CHRIST

To illustrate the fact that the devil never contends for that which is not worthwhile, we shall begin with his devious efforts to destroy the life and/or nullify the ministry of Jesus Christ, the Son of God.

Jesus was perfect and had to be holy and sinless in order to accomplish the purpose for which He was sent into this world. The Bible says, "He was tempted in all points like as we are, yet without sin." (Hebrews 4:15). When Paul wrote Timothy, he stated that Jesus was "justified in the Spirit" (I Timothy 3:16). Although Jesus was clothed in human flesh, He never succumbed to the flesh. He was justified, vindicated, declared righteous by the Spirit. You and I as sinners are justified by faith in the redeeming work of Christ on the cross. However, Christ

---

40   https://thepriceofliberty.org/2019/10/15/eternal-vigilance/Accessed March 23, 2021

Himself needed no such sacrifice of justification, because He was justified in the Spirit. In other words, He was blameless and sinless in His own life.

The sinless, pure life of Jesus Christ is a miracle that the world has seen only once and will never see again. Satan came to tempt Him and discredit Him and condemn Him, but Jesus said, "the ruler of this world is coming, and he has nothing in Me" (John 14:30). "He's got nothing on me" is a common phrase for saying that something or someone has no advantage over or is in no way superior to another person or thing. When Jesus said, "he (Satan) has nothing in me", he was saying that Satan can find no fault, no flaw, no failure in Him. Jesus is the only one who could say that with absolute truthfulness.

The devil, of course, as the archenemy of the Lord Jesus Christ, has done everything in his power to thwart the divine plan of God to redeem a fallen race of people through His only begotten Son. It all started in the book of Genesis when Satan appeared as a slithering snake in the Garden of Eden. God had created Adam and Eve after His image and in His likeness and placed them in a perfect environment. Satan could not be content with what God had created and he became obsessed with disrupting and destroying what God had accomplished in creation. A perfect world was marred by dishonesty, self-ishness, pride, shame, rebellion and, in seemingly no time at all, even murder. God had created something that was good, but Satan tarnished it with his evil plot to sabotage God's master plan. Satan's desire was to soil and spoil the human race to the point that God would have to destroy everything that He had made.

Moses writes: "Then the Lord saw that the wicked-ness of man was great in the earth, and that every intent of the thoughts of his heart was only evil continually. And the Lord was sorry that he had made man on the earth, and He was grieved in his heart. So the Lord said,"" I will destroy man whom I have created from the face of the earth, both man and beast, creeping thing, and the birds of the air, for I am sorry that I have made them"" (Genesis 6:5-7).

However, in the midst of a sinful world God found a man that He could use to save the human race and foil Satan's plan to eradicate it. Noah was the man God chose to use, deemed worthy of grace in God's sight.

Even though God spared humanity from Satan's wicked scheme through Noah's family, it was ultimately necessary for a fallen race to be redeemed from their sinful state. God chose the Jewish people as the ones through whom the Redeemer would come. Consequently, the people of Israel became Satan's target. In Psalm 121:4 the Bible says, "Behold, he who keeps Israel Shall neither slumber nor sleep." God could never afford to sleep concerning Israel, because Satan has forever been on the prowl to undo and destroy God's chosen people. In Genesis 12:1-3, God made some amazing promises to Abraham. He said, "Get out of your country, from your family, and from your father's house to a land that I will show you: I will make you a great nation; I will bless you, and make your name great; and you shall be a blessing. I will bless those who bless you, and I will curse him who curses you: and in you all the families of the earth shall be blessed."

Satan pulled out his bag of tricks in an attempt to concoct a scheme to thwart the plan of God to bring the Messiah through the line of Abraham and Sarah. Sarah was childless into her old age, but eventually, by virtue of a miraculous birth, had the promised son, Isaac, when she was ninety years old, spoiling Lucifer's plan (Genesis 17:17). Then in Exodus

1:15-17 we discover that Satan used Pharaoh as his puppet to subvert God's plan of redemption. He instructed the Egyptian midwives to slay all the boy babies born to Hebrew women but permit their daughters to live. Theologian A. W. Pink states, "It is not difficult to peer behind the scenes and behold one who was seeking to use Pharaoh as an instrument with which to accomplish his fiendish design. Surely, we can discover here an outbreaking of the Serpent's enmity against the Seed of the woman. Suppose this effort had succeeded - what then? Why, the channel through which the promised Redeemer was to come had been destroyed. If all the male children of the Hebrews were destroyed there (would have) been no David, and if no David, no David's Son."[41]

Remember, Satan never contends for anything that is not worthwhile.

In I Samuel 18-19 King Saul, in a twisted state of mind, attempted to kill David multiple times. At first Saul tried to conceal his animosity and jealousy toward David, but eventually he could not camouflage his hatred and became openly zealous in his intention to kill David and anyone he perceived to be David's ally. Saul's devious plot is simply another example of Satan using someone as his pawn to circumvent God's plan of redeeming sinful mankind.

In II Kings 11 the Holy Spirit gives us the story of Athaliah, who was the daughter of Ahab and Jezebel. When she learned that her son, Ahaziah, had been executed by Jehu she seized power over the nation and reigned over the land for six years. Her desire was to eliminate the house of David in Judah; and in an act of vengeance, she rose up to destroy all the royal heirs. Satan would have used this malicious wom-

---

41   Arthur W. Pink, Gleanings in Exodus, (Moody Press, Chicago, 1977), p. 14

an to accomplish his malevolent plan by erasing David's seed from the earth. However, Jehosheba, the daughter of King Joram, sister of Ahaziah, took Joash the son of Ahaziah and hid him in the temple for six years to escape Athaliah's satanically inspired plot to destroy all the royal heirs.

Satan's scheme to eliminate any possibility of the Messiah coming into the world seems unending. In Matthew 2:16 Herod becomes Satan's agent of devastation when he realized he had been outwitted by the Magi and issued an edict to kill all the baby boys in Bethlehem and its vicinity who were two years of age and younger. In Matthew 4 the devil himself attempted to kill Jesus by tempting Him to jump from the pinnacle of the temple. In Luke 4:29 we learn that an enraged crowd in his hometown of Nazareth "led Him (Jesus) unto the brow of the hill whereon their city was built, that they might cast Him down headlong."

On another occasion Satan even used Peter, who was in Christ's inner circle of followers, to discourage Jesus from fulfilling His ultimate mission that was to be accomplished on the cross. Matthew writes, "And Peter took Him aside and began to rebuke Him, saying, 'Far be it from you, Lord; this shall not happen to You.' But He turned and said to Peter, 'Get behind Me, Satan! You are an offense to Me, for you are not mindful of the things of God, but on the things of men.' (Matthew 16:22-23). I can well imagine that Satan was present in the Garden of Gethsemane doing everything in his power to convince Jesus that he should avoid the cross at all costs. Jesus would have none of the devil's malevolent advice and prayed, "O My Father, if it is possible, let this cup pass from Me; nevertheless, not as I will, but as You will" (Matthew 26:39).

SATAN'S EFFORT TO DESTROY THE CHURCH

Today the church of the Lord Jesus Christ has been commissioned to carry on the message of redemption, but the church has been under attack since it was first mentioned by Jesus. When He said, "And I also say to you that you are Peter, and on this rock I will build My church, and the gates of Hades shall not prevail against it" (Matthew 16:18), He promised that the church would be triumphant, but He did not say that the path to victory would be easy. In fact, He indicated that Satan and his minions would do all in their power to undermine and destroy the church.

Adrian Rogers said, "The church is not a showboat, or a cruise ship, but a battleship." The Book of Acts records the beatings, imprisonments, deprivations of Christians and the Neronian persecution of Christians in the first century, and provides frightening examples of Satan attempting to destroy the church in its infancy. History is replete with accounts of Christians being ridiculed, reviled, oppressed and tormented. Today the systematic suppression of Christianity by Communist Party General Secretary Xi Jinping in China and the thousands of Christians who are subjected to unrestrained torture and the mass starvation of believers in North Korean concentration camps give testimony to the fact that Satan is unrelenting in trying to stop the mission of the church.

The devil never ceases to battle the people of God and the church which He bought with the blood of His own Son. If Lucifer finds a smidgeon of vulnerability in the life of a child of God, he will exploit it; and if he discovers that a church is vulnerable in one specific area, he will devise with great craftiness a plan to wreak havoc in that church. Furthermore, if a great denomination with an unparalleled mission force is flourishing, Satan will unleash his heaviest artillery to immobilize that mission force, arrest all evangelism strategies and diminish their influence for good and God.

When Southern Baptists became secure in their glorious victory in the Conservative Resurgence, the god of this world began to explore ways to once again cripple the greatest evangelistic and missionary force in the world. Remember, the devil never contends for anything that is without value; and I am sure he has crafted a myriad of conspiracies for the dismemberment and destruction of the Southern Baptist Convention. Its numerical, financial, educational, evangelistic and missionary strength is too much of a superior target for "the wily one" to ignore. We must all be aware of the subtle devices of the prince of this world. He would like to cripple the SBC mentally, numerically, physically, morally and spiritually in order to stymie or hinder the cause of Christ.

THE PROBLEM OF CARNALITY

First of all, Satan can have a measure of success in his effort to undermine the cause of Christ's eternal kingdom through carnality. I have two definitions for carnality. First, carnality is manifested in a Christian when he or she does not grow up in the nurture and admonition of the Lord. Today we have too many Christians who are walking around in the swaddling clothes of an infantile faith. For example, what would you think if a young woman in your town had a baby that weighted seven pounds and one ounce; and six months later, and one year later and five years later that same baby weighed seven pounds and one ounce? You would say, "Horror of horrors! That is not right. It is not supposed to be that way." Christians are to grow beyond a diet of pablum and milk and begin to feast on the solid food of God's Word, put on the whole armor of God and be filled with the Holy Spirit. Carnal Christians can become more of a liability to the church than an asset, because they do not portray a life of faith and victory.

The second definition of carnality occurs when a Christian lapses into a temporary season of sin. I use the word temporary, because the Bible indicates that no true believer will continue to sin for long. The Apostle John reminds us: "Whoever has been born of God does not sin, for His seed remains in him; and he cannot sin, because he has been born of God" (I John 3:9). In other words, a lost person will leap into sin and love it, but a saved person will lapse into sin and loathe it. A Christian will have moments and perhaps days of carnality, but the Holy Spirit that bears witness to the believer's spirit that he/she is a child of God will also bring such conviction to that individual that they will not be able to remain in that sinful state for long.

More than once I have been a stumbling block to the cause of Christ and the work of redemption because of carnality. Let me provide you with an embarrassing and humiliating example: our three children were teenagers during much of the time that I was pastor of Colonial Heights Baptist Church in Jackson, Mississippi. I have already mentioned that our twin sons are identical, and many people have had trouble distinguishing between the two of them. One winter they were playing basketball. John was number 34 and Jerry was number 35. In this hotly contested game John had four fouls on him near the end of the game and Jerry only had two fouls on him.

My wife and I were in the bleachers watching the game when an opposing player stole the ball from one of our high school players and ran down the court for a lay-up. John, with the four fouls, caught up with him and jumped up to block his shot and hit his hand. The referee blew the whistle and turned to the scorer's table to signal the foul. When he turned his eyes back to the court to identify the offending player John and Jerry had swapped places on the court and Jerry had his hand up indicating that he had committed the foul.

The referee said, "That is a foul on number 35." So, at that point John still had only four fouls and Jerry now had three. They both were still able to remain on the court with less than five fouls. From my vantage point in the stands I stood up, threw up my arms and essentially celebrated the deceitful tactics of my sons who cleverly devised a plan to remain in the game. When I sat down, my wife elbowed me and said, "You hypocrite! How could you possibly endorse that kind of deceptive behavior by your sons?" The Holy Spirit used her to prick my conscience. I began to sheepishly look around to see if anyone noticed my celebratory antics; and everyone was looking at me, even the chairman of my deacons who had a son playing on the opposing team. It was an embarrassing moment with the carnality of the preacher on full display. On the next Sunday morning I explained to my church what I had done and apologized that I had behaved in a way that was unbecoming a Christian.

After that game I began to think, "Is it possible that some lost person saw me reveling in my sons' deception and thought, 'If that is what Colonial Heights Baptist Church is like, I don't need to ever go there.' Or, even worse, someone could have said, "If that is what Christianity is all about, I don't need Christ or His church.' I recalled that Jesus said, "He who is not with me is against me, and he who does not gather with Me scatters abroad" (Matthew 12:30). I became very repentant, because on that night I could very well have scattered or repelled someone from Christ when I should have been gathering people to Christ. I've heard it said that there are two reason why people do not become Christians. First, they have never met a Christian. Second, they have met a Christian. I fear that there have been times when people have observed my life and viewed me as a stumbling block to the Christian faith.

THE PROBLEM OF MEDIOCRITY

We can also hinder the cause of Christ when we resign ourselves to a life of mediocrity and complacency. Many of God's people seem to be satisfied to living a tepid, halfhearted life. Jesus told the parable of the talents in Matthew 25:14-30. In the parable Jesus describes a man who goes on a journey and entrusts his servants with talents (a talent refers to a unit of measurement, generally used to weigh silver or gold). He gives one servant five talents, to another two talents and to yet another one talent. While the first two servants demonstrated good stewardship by investing their talents wisely and winning their master's blessing, the servant who was entrusted only one talent dug a hole in the earth and hid his master's money. His apathy, laziness and insistence on playing it safe resulted in a stern reprimand. His one talent was taken from him and he was thrown out of his master's presence. This steward's life could be described as criminal negligence at worst and indolent mediocrity at best.

Someone asked Dr. R. G. Lee, the great pulpit orator who was pastor of Bellevue Baptists Church in Memphis, the question, "What is mediocrity?" This is what he said:

> "It is a man with locomotive power doing pushcart work. Mediocrity is a man with eagle wings fluttering about like a sparrow instead of soaring into the heavens. Mediocrity is a man with pipe organ abilities making piccolo music for God. Mediocrity is somebody, or anybody, with steam shovel talent doing teaspoon work. Mediocrity is a brilliant artist using his ability to whitewash backyard fences. Mediocrity is a man with oratorical ability spending his time quoting nursery rhymes."[42]

The devil knows that a church member devoted to a mediocre, complacent life will never spoil his demonic plans or obstruct his pathway to destruction. He lures us into thinking that if we can give God the odd moments of our time, the ragged edge of our talents and a trifling trickle of our treasure that will be good enough to soothe our conscience and win God's favor. A Middle English saying is: "faint heart never won fair lady." Likewise, a lukewarm faith never won a victory over Satan.

I'm reminded of the story of Miss Jones, an elderly spinster who lived in a small midwestern community. She had the notoriety of being the oldest resident of the town. One day she died, and the editor of the local newspaper wanted to print a small obituary commemorating Miss Jones's life. However, the more he thought about it the more he became aware that while Miss Jones had never done anything terribly

---

42   Robert G. Lee, Bread from Bellevue Oven, (Sword of the Lord Publishers, Wheaton, Illinois, 1947) p. 129-130

wrong (she had never spent a night in jail or ever been drunk), yet she had never actually done anything of note.

While musing over this the editor went down to have his morning coffee and met the owner of the tombstone establishment in the little community. He poured out his soul to him. The tombstone proprietor stated that he had been having the same problem. He wanted to put something on Miss Jones's tombstone besides: "Miss Nancy Jones, born such-and-such a date and died such-and-such a date," but he couldn't think of anything of significance that she had ever done.

The editor decided to go back to his office and assign the first reporter he came across the task of writing up a small article suitable for both the paper and the tombstone. Upon returning to the office the only fellow around was the sports editor, so he gave him the assignment. They tell me if you pass through that little community you will find the following statement on Miss Jones' tombstone.

Here lies the body of Nancy Jones
For her life held no terrors
She lived an old maid
She died an old maid
No hits, no runs, no errors.

Mediocracy never masters. Complacency never conquers. Apathy never achieves. Lethargy never leads. Indolence is never indomitable.

Although an atheist, Thomas Paine understood the problem of having soldiers who were not fully committed to the American Revolution. In his essay "The Crisis", written on December 23, 1776, he penned:

"These are the times that try men's souls. The summer soldier and the sunshine patriot will, in this crisis, shrink from the service of their country; but he that stands by it now, deserves the love and thanks of man and woman.

Paine continued,

Tyranny, like hell is not easily conquered; yet we have this consolation with us, that the harder the conflict, the more glorious the triumph. What we obtain too cheap, we esteem too lightly: it is dearness only that gives everything its value. Heaven knows how to put a proper price upon its goods; and it would be strange indeed if so celestial an article as freedom should not be highly rated. Britain, with an army to enforce her tyranny, has declared that she has a right (not only to tax) but 'to bind us in all cases whatsoever' and if being bound in that manner, is not slavery, then is there not such a thing as slavery upon earth. Even the expression is impious; for so unlimited a power can belong only to God. [43]

In Paine's reference to "the summer soldier" and "the sunshine patriot," he is referring to soldiers who were committed to the independence of the nation while the days were sunny, and the food was in ample supply and the battles were going well. However, when the war brings bloodshed and demands personal discomfort and sacrifice, these soldiers would retreat, find a safe refuge and be unfaithful to the cause. It's "the summer soldiers" and "the sunshine patriots" that the devil uses to undermine freedom in a nation and victory

---

[43] https://www.ushistory.org/paine/crisis/c-01.htm/ Accessed March 23, 2021

in the church. We are living in a day when self-satisfied mediocracy must be abandoned; and enthusiastic involvement must be embraced.

THE PROBLEM OF COMPROMISE

On the Mount of Temptation, Satan attempted to get Jesus to sin. Using the words of John Phillips, Satan tempted Jesus by offering Him instant food (Matthew 4:3), instant fame (Matthew 4:6) and instant fortune (Matthew 4:8-9). However, the third was a blatant temptation to get Jesus to compromise, to hold alliance with evil. At this point the devil is not trying to lead Jesus to do something for physical comfort such as turning stones to bread to satisfy his hunger for food. Neither is he attempting to get Jesus to do something spectacular which would prove him to be the Son of God and at the same time give him multitudes of followers among men. But in this third temptation Satan urges Christ to compromise. He did not say, "If you are the son of God, I will give you the kingdoms of the world." He said, "All these things will I give thee, if thou wilt fall down and worship me." He made a proposition that if Jesus would worship Him instead of God, he would give Him the kingdoms of this world.

Dr. W. A. Criswell declared,

"To compromise with the world, to love the world, is to repudiate the will of God for our lives. In a dazzling, instantaneous moment, the glories of the kingdoms of this world were flashed before the eyes of the Lord Messiah. Jesus is a king with a kingdom; Satan is a sovereign with

a principality. Why not a treaty? It is possible for them to be rivals no longer. Straighten up. Make peace, make an alliance with evil, accept the help of Satan in the service of God."[44]

In this third temptation Jesus is enticed to gain a temporal, not a spiritual kingdom; tempted to gain it at once, with no cross, no death, no suffering and no sacrifice, tempted to gain by compromise and bribery and homage to evil.

That is what the devil does. He wants us to replace the doctrine of creation with the theory of evolution. He wants us to replace the call to righteousness with the call to relativism. He wants us to replace the exclusivity of the Gospel with the philosophy of universalism. He wants us to replace abstinence with safe-sex, and sobriety with social drinking. He wants us to replace the pro-life agenda with the pro-choice agenda. He wants us to replace our firm convictions with feeble compromise.

Satan wants us to replace the Ten Commandments with the ten suggestions. He wants us to replace the sanctity of marriage with some Hollywood version of co-habitation or with some Supreme Court approved version of same-sex marriage. He wants us to replace love with lust and truth with tolerance. He wants to replace Biblical justice with social justice. He wants us to replace competence with diversity. He wants us to replace "thus saith the Lord" with "thus saith the mind of man." He wants to replace the Kingdom of God with some earthly eat and drink kingdom. He wants us to replace New Testament Christianity with cultural Christianity.

There was no such thing as cultural Christianity in the days of the early church. In fact, to be a Christian was

---

44   W.A. Criswell, Expository Notes of the Gospel of Matthew, (Zondervan Publishing House, Grand Rapids, Michigan, 1961). P. 25

more than likely an assignment for persecution. When Jesus told his disciples to "take up their cross and follow Him", He was inviting them to a death march. However, today the Gospel is often presented as a costless addition to one's life. So today, people add churchgoing to their to-do list, participate in charitable donations to give the appearance of selflessness, wear crosses around their necks to appear pious and check the box next to "Christian" on surveys, all done to give the impression that they are stalwarts of the Christian faith. There are multitudes of people who go through the motions of "accepting Jesus" with no accompanying surrender to His lordship or any significant understanding of His Word.

The compromising church member and the compromising church lacks boldness, is unhealthy, unwise and subject to false teaching.

In the next chapter, I will give you an example of how that may very well be happening to our beloved Southern Baptist Convention. Now please understand, I would like very much to preach a sermon or write a book without attacking error or being argumentative, but when we veer from God's appointed path or when theological problems arise, we must address them – hopefully address them in the spirit of charity.

John Greshem Machen, New Testament scholar and educator, explained,

> "Men tell us that our preaching should be positive and not negative, that we can preach the truth without attacking error. But if we follow that advice, we shall have to close our Bible and desert its teachings. The New Testament is a polemic book almost from beginning to end.... It is when men have felt compelled to take

a stand against error that they have risen to the really great heights in the celebration of the truth."[45]

SATAN'S EFFORT TO DESTROY THE CONVENTION

Satan not only wanted to destroy Christ, and He not only wants to destroy the church, but he also wants to destroy the Convention. Some in Southern Baptist life have been praying for a great awakening in our Baptist Zion, but unfortunately a not-so-great awakening has emerged. Since the Bible is a polemic and uncompromising book, I feel compelled to address the unorthodox "woke" ideology that has infiltrated the evangelical church in recent years. Unfortunately, Southern Baptists have not escaped the infiltration.

While being "woke" may be considered by some as an enlightened and progressive ideology worthy of embracing in the 21st century, others are not nearly so enamored with this movement. It is becoming increasingly apparent that the "awakening" many people are experiencing today is not at all comparable to the Great Awakenings in the 18th and 19th centuries. From time to time, some Southern Baptist leaders have been classified as "woke". There are those who would put Dr. Russell Moore, President of the Ethics and Religious Liberty Commission, in this category. Others would urge him to exercise caution in being identified with the "woke" movement, because it has been linked to those who focus on cancel culture, systemic racism, identity politics and trigger warnings that have incrementally infringed on American's rights. In the December 21, 2016 issue of *Christianity Today*, Dr. Al Mohler referred to Russell Moore as "one of the most brilliant leaders" in this generation; and there is little question as to Moore's

---

45   https://www.azquotes.com/quote/679085/Accessed March 23, 2021

brilliance, but we would do well to pray for God to give him a greater sensitivity to the heartbeat of those who pay his salary. Dr. Moore has been placed in his position to lead, educate, inform and represent Southern Baptists as their public policy advocate, to be the champion of biblical ethics, and to be our liaison to the leadership of the national government.

It is doubtful that Southern Baptists have ever thought of Donald Trump as a paragon of righteousness; and his last month in office was disheartening to many of his staunchest supporters, but during the course of his presidency most of his policies seemed to reflect the ethical standards and guiding principles most evangelicals hold dear. Therefore, it was unwise to refer to Trump supporters as being "on the wrong side of Jesus" and coming from the "Jimmy Swaggart wing" of evangelicalism. The rhetoric of Moore strangely resembles the era of James Dunn of the Baptist Joint Committee on Public Affairs when he offended the ranks of conservatives in the convention by accusing President Reagan of "despicable demagoguery" and "playing politics with prayer."

At the Dallas Convention in 2018 there was a motion made to defund the ERLC, motivated by a concern about Moore's leadership, but the motion was overwhelmingly defeated. On February 18, 2020, the Executive Committee of the SBC approved the formation of a task force to review matters related to the Ethics and Religious Liberty Commission. The Task Force sent out a confidential questionnaire to each executive director of the state/regional conventions. Responses were received from 15 state conventions serving 28,379 congregations, or 60 percent of the churches in friendly cooperation with the SBC. Those churches reported nearly $140,000,000 or 74 percent of total Cooperative Program dollars received by the SBC Executive Committee. No state convention reported that any church had verifiably increased

CP support because of an appreciation for the ERLC. Some conventions reported little or no negative effect from the ministry of the ERLC, while some churches had withheld funds, negatively designated funds, or are considering doing so because of their concerns with the ERLC. Some states reported churches decreasing or even eliminating CP support and some churches have withdrawn funds from the state and national conventions because of a "lack of confidence in many national SBC issues," including concerns about the ERLC.

The Task Force reported on the concerns state executive directors regularly hear from pastors; and listed them without commentary:

1. The open opposition of a candidate for president of the United States

2. The accusation of receiving funding from an organization with ties to George Soros

3. Amicus brief in support of a New Jersey mosque

4. That the ERLC is not available or responsive

5. ERLC stance on immigration

6. Silence on certain issues including timely public support for the religious liberty of California churches during the COVID-19 pandemic

7. The appearance by a recently departed senior staffer on an online panel sponsored by the Joe Biden campaign, contributing to perceptions of a leftward political drift

8. Dr. Moore's stated support of attending homosexual wedding showers and receptions

9. Disrespecting and condescending responses to the questions of messengers. Repeatedly noted was the response given to Pastor John Wofford of Amorel Baptist Church at the 2016 annual meeting

10. That conservative political figures are criticized more frequently and more harshly than moderate to liberal figures.

One large state convention leader summed up his viewpoint by saying, "The ERLC has been a stumbling block not worth the mission dollar investment." The growing unrest over Moore's style of leadership could lead to the same fate experienced by James Dunn in 1991. When Dunn refused to forsake his ideological positions and leadership style for what he called "a mess of politically tainted pottage," the Southern Baptist Convention responded by voting to withdraw all funding for the entity Dunn led, the Baptist Joint Committee. [46]

THE PROBLEM OF CRITICAL RACE THEORY

Initially, "woke" was the term for an "ethnic consciousness" primarily among white college and college-educated activist,and it manifested itself as an awareness of generational wrongs perpetrated by one race against another. The "woke" appear to be compelled to demonstrate they are ethnically conscious through public displays of contrition and through confrontational rhetoric directed at the "non-woke."

Those who understand historical injustices and express concern over the impact they have on current

---

46 https://www.baptiststandard.com/news/baptists/james-dunn-robust-advocate-for-religious-liberty-dies-july-4/Accessed March 23, 2021

inequitable conditions are to be commended. As Christians we understand that no ethnic group is better than other ethnic groups. Biblically speaking, racism is the sin of ethnic partiality or prejudice (James 2:8-9; Leviticus 19:15). As Christians, we know racism is wrong in society, as we are all one race in Adam (Acts 17:26), and especially within the church (Galatians 3:28). Racism is a real sin that should be repudiated by all believers in Christ. Let it be said emphatically that no one has to be "woke" to embrace the biblical imperative to love his/her neighbor.

The original idea of being "woke" was best exemplified by the words of Dr. Martin Luther King, Jr.:

> *"I have a dream that my four little children will one day live in a nation where they will not be judged by the color of their skin but by the content of their character. I have a dream that one day, little black boys and black girls will be able to join hands with little white boys and white girls as sisters and brothers."*[47]

In the civil rights era, being "woke" was indeed about an oppressed people awaking to their birthright of freedom and liberty *as Americans*. It was about engaging in a joint venture of reconciliation with all Americans to secure liberty and justice for all.

It is apparent that "woke" signifies something entirely different today. Justin Stapley, writing for Porter Medium, declares,

> *"Those who speak of themselves as "woke" today are*

---

47   The Report to the SBC Executive Committee by the ERLC Study Committee, (January 16, 2021), p.7

not engaging in a cultural renaissance or movement of reconciliation, liberty, and justice for all. Their language is that of Marxist Sociology and Conflict Theory. When they speak of ethnic or class consciousness, they are not speaking of groups desiring to obtain a birthright of freedom and liberty alongside their brothers and sisters. They're speaking of their belief in a generational struggle between oppressor and the oppressed. This struggle is viewed almost exclusively through the lens of inherent conflict. This conflict, in their view, can only be concluded when social justice is achieved."[48]

At the 2019 Southern Baptist Convention annual meeting in Birmingham there was a resolution introduced that appeared to be inspired by this "woke" ideology. Resolution 9, "On Critical Race Theory and Intersectionality," was not only presented, but also adopted by a large majority of the messengers after a rather vigorous debate. Josh Buice, founder and president of G3 Ministries and pastor of Pray's Mill Baptist Church in Douglasville, GA, wrote an article entitled, "The Woke Tools of the SBC: A Review of Resolution 9," and explained,

"The Southern Baptist Convention fought a 30-year--long battle for the Bible known as the Conservative Resurgence, but what happened in Birmingham, Alabama might just prove to validate the woke movement for the largest protestant denomination in America. . . . A denial of sufficiency will open the door to a new hermeneutic and that will always end in disaster. Anytime the text of Scripture is muzzled by subjective experiences of people—the meaning, method, and message will be

---

48   https://portermedium.com/2019/06/woke-ideology-is-damaging-
-the-fabric-of-society/Accessed March 23, 2021

altered. This is precisely the same broken path traveled by many groups throughout history and in every case, they have all completely capitulated on the authority of God's Word." [49]

In January 2021 Brandon Showalter of the The Christian Post was making reference to Resolution 9 when he wrote, "that the nation's largest Protestant denomination is (becoming) increasingly "woke" and drifting from biblical orthodoxy."[50]

So, what is the infamous Resolution 9, and what are its implications for Southern Baptists?

To begin, a definition of the terms is in order. An analysis of "Critical Race Theory (CRT)" and "Intersectionality" is necessary in order to provide a full understanding of all that is involved. Critical race theory is the view that racism is engrained in the fabric and system of the American society and that our institutions are inherently racist and that race itself, instead of being biologically grounded and natural, is a socially constructed concept that is used by white people to further their personal, economic and political interests at the expense of people of color.

Neil Shenvi, as quoted in an article entitled Critical Race Theory in the Church by Brandon Clay and Frost Smith, defines critical race theory (CTR) as, "an ideology that divides the world into oppressed groups and their oppressors and aims to liberate the oppressed."

The article continues,

---

49   Ibid.

50   https://g3min.org/the-woke-tools-of-the-sbc-a-review-of-resolution-9-on-critical-race-theory-and-intersectionality/Accessed March 23, 2021

Sometimes called 'Cultural Marxism,' CRT borrows concepts from classical Marxism dividing the world into the 'haves' and the 'have nots' and attempts to right the wrongs of previous generations through a redistribution of wealth and power. For instance, CRT teaches some groups, like blacks in America, have been historically oppressed by a dominant white culture. They argue American culture is enmeshed in 'systemic racism' which is a rigged system where African-Americans cannot get justice or fair treatment in 21ˢᵗ century America."

The Oxford Dictionary helps us understand "intersectionality" by explaining that there are many overlapping facets of one's identity and personality that can oppress a person or a group of people. For example, gender, religion, ability, sexuality, race, ethnicity, occupation and degree of education are overlapping identities and the greater the combination of these identities the greater the oppression, at least according to the philosophy of intersectionality. This concept suggests that the more 'oppressed groups' a person is a part of, the more 'oppressed' they are in CRT. For instance, a black lesbian is oppressed while a straight white man is not. According to CRT, the black lesbian is a member of three oppressed groups: she's a woman, she's gay and she's black. She has high intersectionality and should be given more power, whereas a straight white man is a member of none of those historically oppressed groups. In CRT, he has no intersectionality, and his power should be diminished.

Resolution 9 addressed these two viewpoints and created quite a stir among the messengers in Birmingham. The original resolution was presented to the Committee by Stephen Feinstein of Victorville, California. According to Tom

Ascol, the senior pastor of Grace Baptist Church in Cape Coral, Florida, the original resolution was rewritten to say something entirely different from what Feinstein intended. Ascol offered a strong and an appropriate amendment to the resolution, but his amendment was defeated. Ascol stated, "The original resolution clearly denounced Intersectionality and Critical Race Theory as they are typically understood, thus warning Christians against them.[51] Consider Feinstein's original resolution:

> WHEREAS, critical race theory and intersectionality are founded upon unbiblical presuppositions descended from Marxist theories and categories, and therefore are inherently opposed to the Scriptures as the true center of Christian union; and
> WHEREAS, both critical race theory and intersectionality as ideologies have infiltrated some Southern Baptist churches and institutions—institutions funded by the Cooperative Program; and
> WHEREAS, critical race theory upholds postmodern relativistic understandings of truth; and
> WHEREAS, critical race theory divides humanity into groups of oppressors and oppressed, and is used to encourage biblical, transcendental truth claims to be considered suspect when communicated from groups labeled as oppressors;. . ." [52]

---

51 https://www.christianpost.com/news/conservative-baptist-network-launched-amid-woke-trend-in-sbc-emphasizing-scripture-evangelism.html/Accessed March 23, 2021

52 https://founders.org/2019/06/15/resolution-9-and-the-southern-baptist-convention-2019/
Ibid./Accessed March 23, 2021

However, by the time the Resolution Committee had created their own rendition of the original submission, things changed drastically. The Resolution Committee quotes the Baptist Faith and Message 2000 avowing that "All Scripture is totally true and trustworthy," but suddenly makes a left turn saying:

> "WHEREAS, Critical race theory is a set of analytical tools that explain how race has and continues to function in society, and intersectionality is the study of how different personal characteristics overlap and inform one's experience: and, . . .
>
> WHEREAS, Critical race theory and intersectionality alone are insufficient to diagnose and redress the root causes of the social ills that they identify, which result from sin, yet these analytical tools can aid in evaluating a variety of human experiences; . . . therefore be it
>
> RESOLVED, That critical race theory and intersectionality should only be employed as analytical tools subordinate to Scripture – not as transcendent ideological frameworks."[53]

While the resolution places CTR and Intersectionality as subordinate to God's Word, it specifically states multiple times that these ideologies can be used as analytical tools to aid in interpretating the human experience and presumably the Bible as well. While the resolution affirms the infallibility of God's Word it appears to cast doubts about the sufficiency of Holy Scripture, especially for understanding the human condition.

---

53   https://www.sbc.net/?s=resolution+on+critical+race+theory+and+intersectionality/Accessed March 23, 2021

Ascol challenged the Resolution Committee, correctly explaining that both CRT and Intersectionality are "rooted in ideologies that are incompatible with Christianity."

Western history has depended on objective truth to develop the principles by which our society has been established, but those who have become "woke", either knowingly or unknowingly are seeking to re-envision the way our society is to be seen. There is ample evidence to show that they have their roots in a secular Marxist worldview and its origin in the Frankfurt School. The Frankfurt School was a movement of the far-left European philosophers who sought to apply the ideas of Karl Marx in a social context. The Frankfurt School rejected objective truth and taught that knowledge is strictly embedded in serving human interests; and therefore, cannot be considered value neutral and objectively independent. All subject matter becomes an element of interpretation and can be manipulated to serve a purpose and breeds things like CRT, Intersectionality, identity politics and social justice. [54]

The average Southern Baptist may think Marxism died with the collapse of the Soviet Union. The Marxist movement left untold millions dead, but the philosophies and conditions that led to its rise still exist today. John Andrews, former vice president of Colorado Christian University, explains,

"Far from being forgotten and irrelevant, Marx's ideas pervade key institutions, from universities and schools, to mass media and popular entertainment, to major cor-

---

54   https://www.americanthinker.com/articles/2019/03/marxism_the_ frankrt_school_and_the_leftist_takeover_of_the_college_campus. html/Accessed March 23, 2021

porations and medicine, to the arts and sciences. They've even seeped into many churches and seminaries."[55]

Kevin McCullough, radio host for Salem Media NYC and syndicated columnist, explains,

"Woke-ism is selfish, it can't see past its own circle of feelings, and it is causing the American church to shrink to an ineffective level. It's defanging the power that God has given it to be used for good, and to advance His kingdom on earth."[56]

In December 2020 Southern Baptist Seminary presidents, recognizing the controversy prompted by Resolution 9, weighed in on the issue by saying that Critical Race Theory is incompatible with the denomination's central statement of faith. Daniel Akin, president of Southeastern Baptist Theological Seminary agreed that the theory had its origin in Marxism, stating, "Since Marxist theories are atheistic, Southern Baptists must reject its underlying framework for understanding the world."

The six presidents stated,

"We stand together on historic Southern Baptist condemnations of racism in any form and we also declare that affirmation of critical race theory, intersectionality

55   https://thefederalist.com/2020/07/07/if-we-dont-stop-it-marxism--will-annihilate-the-american-way-of-life/Accessed March 23, 2021

56   https://townhall.com/columnists/kevinmccullough/2020/11/19/the--woke-church-is-failing-its-mission-n2580376/Accessed March 23, 2021

and any version of critical race theory is incompatible
with the Baptist Faith and Message."[57]

In January 2015 Dwight McKissic, Sr., pastor of Cornerstone Baptist Church in Arlington, Texas, reacted to Resolution 9 and other issues in a blog entitled "We are Getting Off the Bus." Referring to the statement issued by the six seminary presidents, McKissic stated,

"This could be used as grounds to dis-fellowship (any church opposed to the Council of Seminary Presidents statement) from the SBC or dismiss professors from their teaching assignments. I am not willing to concede that type of power to the SBC/CSP based on an academic policy that originated with six Anglo seminary presidents."

He admitted that he had expressed a keen interest in withdrawing membership from the Southern Baptist Texas Convention in 2006 over several issues but remained affiliated with the state convention until the SBTC adopted a "strongly worded, anti-CRT policy in early 2021. The newly adopted policy was the last piece of evidence McKissic needed to break ties with the SBTC and act on the decision he had made in 2006.

In announcing his decision to depart the SBTC, the Cornerstone pastor affirmed,

"the Bible speaks with supreme authority in every area, including race. Where any racial theory contradicts

---

57   https://www.baptiststandard.com/news/baptists/southern-baptist-seminary-presidents-nix-critical-race-theory/Accessed March 23, 2021

Scripture, Scripture rules over all. This is applicable to the Council of Seminary Presidents and the SBC Critical Race Theory kerfuffle." But then he added, . . . "If the Council of Seminary Presidents/Southern Baptist Convention policy is ratified in June, we are discontinuing our affiliation with the SBC... We are getting off the bus."[58]

While many Baptists love Pastor McKissic and appreciate his convictions and courage to express them, there are others who vehemently disagree with his position on certain issues. This became evident not many days after he published his blog, "We Are Getting Off the Bus." For example, John V. Rutledge, who identified himself as a former Southern Baptist, wrote McKissic and stated, "the Southern Baptist Convention has been repenting (foolishly) of the 'sin' of whiteness and has rebaptized itself as an exemplar of diversity." Rutledge referred to African Americans as "Negroes" and "savages."[59]

SBC President J.D. Greear responded to the caustic letter by saying he was "infuriated. This attitude is anti-Gospel and should be treated as such." Ronnie Floyd, president and CEO of the SBC Executive Committee admitted that he was glad Rutledge had left the SBC 20 years earlier. Floyd tweeted, "It is best he did, because the words and spirit of his letter to (McKissic) does not represent us at all. It is contradictory to our "Baptist Faith and Message" and our commitment to human dignity."[60]

Our Father in heaven said it best in I John 4:7: "Beloved, let us love one another, for love is of God; and everyone

---

58   https://dwightmckissic.wordpress.com/Accessed March 23, 202

59   https://www.baptistpress.com/resource-/Accessed March 23, 2021

60   library/news/racist-letter-sent-to-black-pastor-condemned-as-vile--sick-and-disgusting/Accessed March 23, 2021

who loves is born of God and knows God. He who does not love does not know God, for God is love." Unfortunately, the letter written to McKissic and the responses to the letter only illustrates the racial tension that still exists among some.

I am convinced that the Resolution Committee likely had every good intention of presenting a resolution that would be informative and helpful, but the very mention of anything connected to a Marxist philosophy being an analytical tool for our understanding of the human experience is frightening.

There is evidence that this dangerous philosophy is extending its tentacles into our institutions of higher learning and some of our agencies and is a startling example of conformity to the world. As Southern Baptists we must not glide past the Marxists fingerprints that are evident all over our current turmoil in politics, education and the church. We may look at "the cancel culture", "the left" or "the wokeness" and dismiss it all as a passing fad. If it is only a fad, we can be sure that the devil is already concocting another poisonous cocktail for us to drink and we are all vulnerable to what he offers up at his shady, suspicious, seductive saloon. And when people begin to figure out the problems of Critical Race Theory, Satan will come up with another scheme to tempt every believer to compromise the truth of God's Word.

Mike Stone, pastor of Emmanuel Baptist Church in Blackshear, Georgia, and an announced candidate for Southern Baptist Convention president in 2021, preached at Mid- America Baptist Theological Seminary for a conference sponsored by the Conservative Baptist Network and reminded us that there is but one incontrovertible source of truth. His message was entitled, "My Analytical Tool" and his text was II Timothy 3: 16-17. In his message he underscored the sufficiency of Scripture and proclaimed that the Bible was altogether adequate in and of itself. He declared,

> "If we believe that every word is inspired, if we believe those words have meaning, if we believe that meaning can be derived from sound hermeneutics, led by the Spirit of God, then we should be troubled that among our Southern Baptist leadership there is the increasing thought that we cannot interpret the Biblical text unless we have writers and commentaries on our shelves of various ethnicities, cultures, gender and background."

Stone continued,

> "Recently in a prominent Zoom conference call about race relations in our Southern Baptist Zion, one guest said he was hopeful for a day when 'it will not be black faces with white voices or black faces with predominately white theology.' The Georgia Baptist pastor added, "The suggestion that there is a white theology, and a black theology is just plain bad theology. There is not a theological truth for those who are black and another for those who are women and another for those who are men and another one for those who are American and another for those who are non-American. Yes, we should be troubled that one noted professor in one of our seminaries told his class, "If you don't know it yet, if all you have is males reading the Scriptures you have a very, very misinterpreted Bible. I need sisters within the body of Christ who can help me to read the Scripture in ways in which my maleness is preventing me from reading it.' He went on to say the same thing about being white, about being an American, about being a

graduate of a certain institution, and even about the limitations of understanding the text because we live in the 21st century.

"If our ethnicity, gender or personal experiences cause us to see something differently in the text, these are biases that should be rejected and fought, not embraced and furthered. You can call that standpoint hermeneutics if you want to, but the best word you can call it is "error". And it is more appropriate for a Benny Hinn crusade than a Southern Baptist Seminary."

Stone concluded his sermon by thundering,

"There has been an awful lot of talk since the Birmingham convention about whether or not we need a new analytical tool. I have come tonight to tell you that you and I have already got one and it is very, very old. It is my Bible, your Bible, our analytical tool."

Resolution 9 was adopted by the convention messengers who may have approved it because they were ill informed about the issues involved. However, regardless of their possible naivety, the vote revealed Satan's encroachment, the church's vulnerability, and the necessity for perennial vigilance for the cause of Christ. Among all his weapons, Lucifer is using carnality, mediocrity, compromise, and Critical Race Theory to advance his malevolent purpose on this earth.

Jesus was tempted three times in the wilderness by Satan and each time our Lord responded, "It is written!" The mention of the word of God thwarted the devil's onslaughts. His Word must be our firm foundation today and in every age.

CHAPTER 4 ➡

THE CHURCH GROWTH MOVEMENT

EVERY SINCERE, GOD CALLED PASTOR wants to see the church he serves grow; and he will use every legitimate, biblical practice and procedure to see his church flourish and mature spiritually and numerically. The book of Acts informs us that the New Testament church grew rapidly and exponentially.

God is not vague as to what His church is to be like. Through the Bible, God gives us ample information about the foundation of the church (Matthew 16:13-20), how men are to lead the church (Acts 6:1-7, Titus 1:5-9, I Timothy 3:1-13, Ephesians 4:11), how the redeemed are to live (Romans 12:1-2, Galatians 2:20, Colossians 1:10, I Peter 2:21), (Matthew 5:13-16), the ordinances of the church (I Corinthians 11), the worship of the church (Acts 20:7, Acts 2:42), the taking of the offering (Colossians 3:16), and how we can be used of the Lord to grow the church (Matthew 28:18-20, Acts 1:8).

However, as we begin to think about the fall of the Conservative Resurgence, we must remember that Satan is always insidiously working to hinder the work of God and he seldom uses an open, obvious, frontal attack. Although it seems like he is less discrete in his vicious attacks, he has not yet attempted to openly destroy the church or demonstrate an obvious hatred for the work of God, at least in our United States experience. Rather, he is subtle and indirect in his destructive strategies. He has his spurious, counterfeit plots and schemes to undermine and sabotage God's work through the church.

In Exodus 7 we have an example of Satan's devises and power. In verse one the Bible says, "So the Lord said to Moses: See, I have made you as God to Pharaoh, and Aaron your brother shall be your prophet." Moses was to be God's ambassador with divine authority and gifted to perform miracles. When Moses and Aaron appeared before Pharaoh, Moses told Aaron to cast down his rod. When Aaron did so, it became a serpent. This miracle was designed to convince the Egyptian ruler that he should permit the Israelites to leave the land of bondage.

In response to the miracle wrought by God through Moses and Aaron, Pharaoh called for his wise men and sorcerers, who were also magicians, and they duplicated the miracle by casting down their rods and turning them into serpents. In commenting on this passage, Arthur Pink writes, "The sad thing is that so many of the professed servants of God have, instead of faithfully maintaining the integrity of God's Word, attempted to blunt its keen edge in order to make it more acceptable to the carnal mind."[61] However, those who believe in the infallibility of God's Word, find no need to doubt or

---

61   Arthur W. Pink, Gleanings in Exodus (Moody Press, Chicago, 1977) p. 54

debate the validity of this miracle. It happened as the Bible says, and the serpent produced when Aaron cast down his rod swallowed up the serpents of Pharaoh's magicians. This fascinating narrative in Exodus 7 illustrates that, for every work of God, the arch-deceiver has a substitute or a counterfeit. When it comes to starting and growing a church, Satan masquerades as an angel of light to provide alternatives to what the Bible teaches about ecclesiology, that is, the nature, structure and growth of the church

In the 1970s, a church growth movement emerged that began to promote a seeker sensitive, felt needs, consumer-driven emphasis in churches across America. Some embraced this movement and developed it into a philosophy of ecclesiology emphasizing that "the ends justified the means." It was a pragmatic approach to church growth that promoted a "whatever works" mentality. Many churches grew numerically, and no one seemed to recognize that there is a difference between what the world calls success and what the Bible calls surrender. In this chapter we will discuss the influence of pragmatism on the church growth movement and the emergent church.

PRAGMATISM

Pragmatism surfaced in the United States in the late nineteenth century and has its origins in the teachings of John Stuart Mill, one of the most influential thinkers throughout the history of classical liberalism. Mill had a significant influence on John Dewey, who applied pragmatism to education, and William James, who applied it to religion. James believed that the way to determine truth was to examine practical results. He insisted that only those things that are beneficial and help move us in the right direction are worthwhile. In essence the question for the pragmatist is not, "Is it true; or is it right?" but rather, "Does it produce the desired results?" For the pragmatist, there is no objective truth; "it is reduced to an idea that has worked in practical experience."[62]

It would appear that the philosophy of William James, whether intentional or accidental, helped shape some of the concepts of the church growth movement that emerged in the 20th century. That movement can be traced to Donald McGavran, who has been described as an unabashed pragmatist, and to the School of World Missions at Fuller Theological Seminary in Pasadena, California. McGavran, who had served as a missionary in India, reportedly formulated the main principles of Church Growth theory in the 1930s, but it was not until the 1970s with the publishing of his book, *Understanding Church Growth* that his principles began to be applied in churches across America.

C. Peter Wagner, professor of church growth at Fuller School of World Missions, is Donald McGavran's best-known student and has avowed that "consecrated pragmatism" does not allow compromise of doctrine or ethics, but at the same time has stated, "We ought to see clearly that the end does justify the means. If the method I am using accomplishes the goal I am aiming at, it is for that reason it is a good method. If, on the other hand, my method is not accomplishing the goal, how can I be justified in continuing to use it."[63] "If the goal of church growth is numerical

---

62 Funk and Wagnalls Encyclopedia, CD-ROM 1995 version, "John Dewey."

63 C. Peter Wagner, Leading Your Church to Growth (Regal, Ventura, California, 1984), p. 161

growth with no biblical warrant, it is moving biblical exposition out of Christian ministry and replacing it with vaudeville." [64]

The fact that Robert Schuller, former pastor of the Crystal Cathedral in Anaheim, California, claimed to be the founder of the church growth movement may be debatable, but there is no doubt that he was among the very first pastors to implement the principles articulated by McGavran. Schuller stated, "My particular job as senior pastor is, hopefully, to deliver messages that will bring great crowds of people to church on Sunday morning. . . It is my job to attract non-churched people into the sanctuary on Sunday mornings through sermons that do not sound like sermons, but which sound like helpful and inspiring messages." [65] He also added, "Inspiring preaching much be backed up by exciting programs to impress the unchurched people of every age." [66] In his book, *Your Church Has Real Possibilities*, Schuller proclaims that one of the most spiritual experiences of his life came from the musical production, *Man from La Mancha.*

Bill Hybels, pastor of Willow Creek Community Church in South Barrington, Illinois, and Rick Warren, pastor of Saddleback Church, a megachurch affiliated with the Southern Baptist Convention in Lake Forest, California, became leaders of the "church growth movement" and their influence began to spread throughout the evangelical world, including many churches in the Southern Baptist Convention. For example, Warren's pragmatic approach to growing his church became evident in his statement, "I contend that

---

64   https://www.apprising.org/2010/07/10/fuller-theological-seminary-birthed-church-growth-movement/Accessed March 23, 2021

65   Robert H. Schuller, Your Church has Real Possibilities, (Regal Books Division, Glendale, California, 1974), p. 60

66   Ibid., p. 141

when a church continues to use methods that no longer work, it is being unfaithful to Christ."[67] Whether right or wrong, Warren's methods have produced one of the most influential mega churches in America.

Pragmatism is defined by the *Cambridge Dictionary* as "the quality of dealing with a problem in a sensible way that suits the conditions that really exist, rather than following fixed theories, ideas, or rules."[68] In pragmatism it is easy to conclude that the results justify the means, but we must never believe that success is necessarily indicative of faithfulness to God's Word. In fact, pragmatism is a very dangerous alternative to Scripture. This is when we forget all about truth and simply look for whatever works. If the Bible does not work, pragmatists set it aside for *The Power of Positive Thinking* or *The Purpose Driven Church*, some self-help concept or something that does work. If we were to take that to the extreme we might say, "If we can create more involvement and excitement with strobe lights, theatrical fog and the pastor coming onto the platform on a zipline rather than from his prayer closet, then we will go with the strobe lights, the theatrical fog and the zipline."

One blogger asserts, "The obvious danger of pragmatism in the church is that we lose our focus on the absolute standard God has given us in His Word. When we lose that focus the church is on a slippery slope to becoming like the world. When we discard God's standards we must depend on our own deeply flawed standards. We begin to trust in our-

---

67   Rick Warren, The Purpose Driven Church (Zondervan Publishing House, Grand Rapids, Michigan, 1995) p. 65

68   https://www.oxfordlearnersdictionaries.com/definition/english/pragmatism. Accessed April 6, 2021

selves and lose our trust in God."[69] Another writer called pragmatism the church's kryptonite, because the building blocks of pragmatism are strategies, models, and techniques culled not from the scriptures, but from the world of business.[70]

When I became the pastor of Eastside Baptist Church in Marietta, Georgia, in 1994 the membership had been influenced by the philosophy of Hybels and Warren. Most of the staff were committed to the kind of "church growth movement" that was reflected in those ministries. I

> I COULD NOT HELP BUT WONDER IF ALL THEIR ON-STAGE PRODUCTIONS, CLEVER VIDEO PRESENTATIONS, AND ACCOUTREMENTS OF RELIGIOUS RITUAL INDICATED SOME DEGREE OF DOUBT ABOUT THE SUFFICIENCY OF SCRIPTURE.

went on an exploration expedition to Willow Creek one weekend to experience their conference for pastors and their worship services in order to better understand their philosophy of growing a church. I was impressed in many ways by the production and efficiency of the conference. Their music was "performed" with excellence. They had a dramatic production that was humorous, entertaining and with a relevant moral lesson. The production was a spectacle worthy of the ecclesiastical equivalent of an academy award. The church's spacious auditorium was filled to capacity and the sermon was masterfully communicated by Hybels. But at the conclusion, there was no appeal for a public decision. There was something

---

69 https://www.challies.com/articles/challenges-to-the-church-pragmatism/Accessed March 23, 2021

70 https://www.challies.com/articles/challenges-to-the-church-pragmatism/Accessed March 23, 2021

in my spirit that was unsettling about the worship experience, and the church's doctrine of ecclesiology, and maybe even the doctrine of soteriology. I could not help but wonder if all their on-stage productions, clever video presentations, and accoutrements of religious ritual indicated some degree of doubt about the sufficiency of Scripture.

Dr. Danny Akin, now president of Southeastern Baptist Theological Seminary, was also there that weekend. Near the end of the conference I asked him to share his observations with me. He had been equally impressed with much of what he had experienced but had a list of nine things which were somewhat disturbing to him. As I look back on that experience now, I suspect that the Willow Creek church was greatly influenced by pragmatism. What they were doing was obviously successful, but there was a question in my mind about whether their methods were based on biblical truth or on strategies, models and techniques culled from the world of business and entertainment.

As we think about the church growth emphasis of the last quarter of the 20th century there are several evidences of pragmatism we need to consider that became an integral part of that movement.

MARKETING THE CHURCH

Obviously, every church has a DNA and a special identity, and there is nothing wrong with using logos, websites, social media, bulletins, newsletters, signs and mailers to inform people about your church and what it has to offer. However, at Eastside I was introduced to a level of marketing that was mostly foreign to me. At one of my first staff meetings at Eastside one of the members of our team, who was infatuated with the Willow Creek Church, asked me, "Pastor, we need a target audience in order to effectively market our church. Who do you want that target audience to be?" I was not even sure I understood the question. I said, "Our city is a suburb of Atlanta. Marietta has a population of over 50,000 people. There are probably 20,000 people within a five-mile radius of our church. Our target audience is everyone within that five-mile radius and beyond." Prior to the church growth movement, every pastor I knew would have given such an answer. The words "target audience" would have never been used, but each of us who were pastors in that day would have immediately known that our mission field was every person within a certain radius of our church building.

However, the staff wanted to know what specific demographic, what age group, what economic segment of the county I intended for the church to try to reach. In the course of our discussion, I discovered that the staff apparently wanted to reach the group who where then called YUPPIES (the young, upwardly mobile professionals) in our area. That was difficult for me to swallow for two reasons. First, I simply wanted to reach the lost, regardless of whether they were rich or poor, black or white, in the majority or minority, educated or uneducated, Democrats or Republicans, liberals or conservatives, passionate or lukewarm, tall or short, introverts or extroverts, professionals or hourly-wage earners, leaders or followers, healthy or infirmed. Secondly, I was 53 years old when I was called to the church and not sure that my age and style of ministry would appeal to the specified affinity group the staff wanted to target.

So, quickly it became crystal clear to me that the staff was looking for an affinity group to whom they could market the church. I began to investigate the mantras and principles of churches that were committed to a marketing strategy. They were both astonishing and puzzling to me. I was reading things like:

- *"A church for people who aren't into church."*
  - *"We're not your grandma's church."*
- *"It is critical that we keep in mind a fundamental principle of Christian communication (or marketing): the audience, not the message, is sovereign."*
- *"The Bible is one of the world's great marketing texts."*
- *"Marketing is essential for a business or a church to operate successfully."*
- *"The Bible does not warn about the evils of marketing."*
- *"Think of your church, not as a religious meeting place, but as a service agency."*

As I reviewed some of these marketing slogans and concepts, I began to wonder, "If you are inviting people to church who aren't into church, are you inviting them to something that is the antithesis of church." And as I look back on the church growth movement I must ask: "What has been accomplished by removing grandma from the premises of the local church?" "And in marketing the church, if the audience, not the message is sovereign, is not the primary goal to get a crowd rather than a convert?" I began to question, "Is it our job to woo people into the church as satisfied customers or win people to Christ as a part of His body?"

I soon discovered that while the pastor search committee indicated they were looking for a pastor, it appeared that the staff was looking for a CEO, a "vision caster" and a leader. They gave me books like Peter Drucker's book on "Managing the Non-Profit Organization ", and Steven Covey's book on "The 7 Habits of Highly Effective People", and John Maxwell's book on "Developing the Leader Within You". I began to feel like I needed an MBA (Master of Business Administration) from Harvard or a marketing degree from the University of Pennsylvania. I did not have a degree in business or marketing, but a degree in theology; and my experience had not been in salesmanship or supervision, but in Christian ministry and preaching the Gospel.

Now, I am intelligent enough to know how you identify an affinity group and develop your marketing strategy around them. I am a senior citizen, and when my wife and I watch television it is usually around lunch time or supper time. The programs we watch during those restful hours are typically *The Andy Griffith Show, Walker - Texas Ranger, I Love Lucy* and *Gunsmoke*. Apparently, these programs are targeting senior adults, because the advertisers are for hearing aids, reverse mortgages, walk-in tubs, burial insurance, and Medicare/Medicaid. And even though I had some understanding of carving out an affinity group and essentially targeting that one segment of society for our church's outreach program, that philosophy of ministry seemed to stand out as a direct contradiction to the Lord's command to take the Gospel to the whole world.

I knew that I did not want to be driven by pragmatism and allow marketing to be the primary method we used to grow our church. I knew that "a Madison Avenue" approach to making the church visible and attractive to an affinity group might produce results, but I was convinced that good results were not necessarily indicative of faithfulness to Scripture. I also believed that it was more important for me to fill the pulpit than to fill the pew; and that if we were to fill the pews we needed to do so, primarily, by means of mobilizing the church to share the Gospel as commanded and make disciples.

I refused to believe that preaching is an antiquated, outdated, outmoded method of communicating the Gospel or that we should replace the sermon with dialogue, films, panel discussions, dramatic presentations and concerts. While a church may use these methods of communicating truth, they should be supplemental, and even incidental, to the preaching of the Gospel. I agree with the pastor who proclaimed, "If the church is alive, it is because the pulpit is alive – and if a church is dead, it is because the pulpit is dead!"

Pragmatism in the Church Growth movement relies on man's wisdom more than God's wisdom. At the Georgia Baptist Evangelism Conference, a preacher stated that he was in a conversation with a church planter who had surveyed the people in the community where he planned to start a new church. In the survey he asked the individuals in the community five questions. They were: (1) Are you actively attending any church? (2) Why do you think most people don't attend church? (3) What kind of pastor do you think would best serve the needs of this community? (4) What kind of needs do you have that a church might help you resolve? (5) What kind of church would be attractive and inviting to you?

Why would we consult the unchurched to find out what they want to hear from a preacher and what they would like to experience in a church? Isn't the church supposed to be a place where God speaks to the world, through His Word proclaimed from the pulpit?

I've read that *The New Yorker* magazine once posted the following:

The preacher, instead of looking out upon the world, looks out upon public opinion, trying to find out what the public would like to hear. Then he tries his best to duplicate that and bring his product into a marketplace in which others are trying to do the same. The public, turning to our culture to find out about the world, discovers there is nothing but its own reflection. The unexamined world, meanwhile, drifts into the future.

We need to be sensitive to the needs of a lost and dying world, but church planters need to be careful about giving lost and unchurched people too much input into what should characterize a local church. Our Lord is the author and founder of the church and He should be the one who is the architect of its theology, the designer of its mission and the One who establishes the requirements for its membership. The best church growth book in existence is the book of Acts; and the ingredients for church growth in that blessed book of the New Testament outlines God's prescription for establishing and growing a church. The church must be built upon absolute truth, not experimental guesses authored by individuals in a vain attempt to duplicate the positive things happening in their lives.

SUBJECTIVISM

In addition to the problem of pragmatism and the marketing of the church derived from that, another culprit in the church growth movement is subjectivism. Subjectivism has been defined as the philosophical tenet that suggests that our own mental activity or personal viewpoint is the only unquestionable fact of our experience. Subjectivism has its philosophical basis in the writings of the French scientist and philosopher, René Descartes, and has been condemned by most Christian theologians. However, the enemy has clandestinely introduced this vain philosophy into multitudes of churches. In essence, subjectivism is the ideology which suggests that something may be true for you, but not for me.

We live in a day of subjectivism, relativism, tolerance and philosophical pluralism, a day of "individualized moral menus." Thus, when we have a "whatever-I'm-feeling" morality, the individual becomes the authority over the government, the laws of the land, the church, the Bible and even God. It is like the day in the Book of Judges when "there was no king in Israel; everyone did what was right in his own eyes" (Judges 21:25).

One famous example occurred when President Barak Obama was asked to give his definition of sin. He said, "Sin is when I am out of alignment with my own values." That, my friend, is subjectivism!

Subjectivism is a part of the humanistic philosophy that puts man at the center of the universe; and man, not God becomes the authority for all things. Subjectivism is all about the deifying of man and the humanizing of God. And forty to fifty years ago this philosophy gave rise to the seeker-sensitive, felt-needs, consumer-friendly ingredients of the church growth movement. There is no doubt that many who bought into this movement did so without realizing the deceptive elements of this philosophy.

Unfortunately, the seeker sensitive movement missed the mark with its man-centered focus. We are told that almost everything seekers know comes through thirty-second sound-bytes and brief discourses; and those who create a worship service for them typically try to design a fast-paced program with soft doctrine, inspirational music and compelling drama sprinkled with humor. They also want to make sure that they provide a comfortable, attractive, inviting and non-threatening environment for those who attend their church services. John H. Armstrong, writing for the Alliance of Confessing Evangelicals, commented, "The (church growth) movement has an aggressively strong commitment to use of the social sciences such as sociology, psychology and anthropology, holding the Bible in one hand and the social sciences with the other, all the time affirming, 'All truth is God's truth.'"[71]

While a non-threatening worship experience may sound appealing to an unchurched individual, it seems almost antithetical to the ministry of Jesus Christ. In John 6 Jesus preached to multitudes of people. It is doubtful that his message was seeker friendly because the Bible says, "from that time many of His disciples went back and walked with Him no more" (John 6:66). In John 10 the message of Jesus enraged the people to the extent that they wanted to kill Him (John 10:27-31). The Jews responded the same way in John 8:58-59 when Jesus said, "Most assuredly, I say to you, before Abraham was, I am." Furthermore, Jesus indicated that those who serve Him will be maligned and persecuted (Matthew 10:25). He also declared that He did not come to bring peace, but a sword (Matthew 10:34). Therefore, if we craft a worship service that is non-threatening and preach sermons that pacify and placate, are we presenting a true image of Christian discipleship?

Can an unredeemed person ever actually feel comfortable in church, which is the body of Christ? Adrian Rogers once stated, "When people come hear me preach, I want them to leave either mad, sad or glad." I suppose the "mad"

---

71   https://www.gotquestions.org/seeker-sensitive-church.html p.1
     Ibid., p.2/Accessed March 23, 2021

would represent those who simply did not like the message of a preacher committed to declaring the truth of God. The "sad" perhaps would represent those who came under conviction but did nothing about it. The "glad" would signify those who heard the truth, agreed with it and celebrated it. One source explained, "The preaching of the Gospel brings discomfort to those who are outside the fold of God, and those who attempt to circumvent discomfort are not being loving. In fact, just the opposite is true. If we love someone, we want him to know the truth about sin, death, and salvation so we can help him avoid an eternity in hell." [72]

Dr. Roy Fish, who for years was the distinguished emeritus professor of evangelism at Southwestern Baptist Theological Seminary, was the interim pastor at Eastside Baptist Church in Marietta before I became the pastor there. When I was praying over whether or not I should accept the call to become the pastor of the church, I called Dr. Fish and asked, "Would you please describe the Eastside Baptist Church for me." He replied, "I can describe it in a sentence. It is a seeker friendly church with no seekers."

The seeker-sensitive movement is based on the belief that there are countless numbers of people in our cities and towns who have a great desire to know God, but their perspective about "grandma's church" turns them off and repels them from faith in Christ. However, is that really true? The Bible says, "There is none who understands; There is none who seeks after God" (Romans 3:11). There is no way that rebellious sinners can initiate their own salvation. In I Corinthians 2:14 the Apostle Paul writes, "But the natural man does not receive the things of the Spirit of God, for they are foolishness

---

72 https://www.gotquestions.org/emerging-church-emergent.html/ Accessed March 23, 2021

to him; nor can he know them, because they are spirituality discerned." In other words, the unsaved person does not seek God, because he doesn't recognize his need for Him.

However, God is at work to win our hearts and we should rest in the assurance that God pursues us. He never gives up on us. He never let's go of us, because He loves us and because He is faithful. God is the seeker and in Ezekiel 34:11 we find these words: "For thus says the Lord God, "Indeed, I Myself will search for My sheep and seek them out." In John 4:23 and John 6:44 Jesus emphatically informs us that it is God who is the seeker. God doesn't just answer when we call. He is taking the initiative. He is the one going on a quest for the human heart. And in Luke 19:10 we are informed that Jesus is the One who "came to seek and save the lost."

To be truthful, there are many "seeker" churches that have accomplished much in the work of God; some of them have grown exponentially and are now mega churches. These churches have claimed an enormous number of conversions and drawn multitudes of unchurched people into their membership. The pastors of these churches have gained great popularity and developed magnificent programs for children and students. For every soul genuinely saved in these churches and for every life that has been transformed by the power of the Gospel we all give thanksgiving and praise to our God, because any exposure we can give the unsaved to the Gospel is a great thing. However, many of these churches have a shell of the truth but is empty of the truths of sin, judgment, hell and the holiness of God and the surrender He requires. Furthermore, all things must be judged by the measuring rod of God's infallible Word; and the questions must be asked, "Dare we add or subtract anything from the Word of God? Is the Bible completely sufficient?"

The church growth movement began to fade away, but it was followed by an even more dangerous enemy: the emergent church movement. Bailey Smith persistently asked, "What is the emergent church emerging from and what it is emerging to?" I think his questions were appropriate. Those of us who grew up in the 1950s remember when the churches were growing and had great influence in the community, when we had two-week revivals and two-week Vacation Bible Schools, when our public schools had chapel services with local pastors preaching the sermons with all students and faculty present. Dr. Smith would ask, "Who wants to emerge from that?"

The proponents of the emergent church contend that as culture changes, a new church should emerge in response. One writer states,

> "Post-modernism can be thought of as a dissolution of 'cold, hard fact' in favor of 'warm, fuzzy subjectivity.' The emerging/emergent church movement can be thought of the same way. . . .[(This movement] falls into line with basic post-modernist thinking – it is about experience over reason, subjectivity over objectivity, spiritually over religion [faith], images over word, outward over inward, feelings over truth." [73]

Now, in addition to the church growth movement and the emergent church movement we have entered into the era of the church as a counterculture which deals with identity, purpose and organization, and forces a redefinition of categories like religion, education and politics both sacred and secular. The counter-culture phenomenon will very likely

---

73   https://www.sunypress.edu/p-3189-the-church-as-counterculture. aspx/Accessed March 23, 2021

challenge the church to examine its perspectives on war and genocide, racism and nationalism, and the legitimacy of classical liberalism and capitalism. This is a relatively new movement and provides more questions than answers, but it illustrates that the devil is always attempting to find new ways to denigrate believers, diminish the ministry of the church and destroy the Christian enterprise. [74]

Because of those who question the infallibility and sufficiency of the Word of God, the influence of the church growth movement, and philosophies that militate against our faith, we must stand fast against the wiles of the devil.

G. K. Chesterton once said, "To keep a white fence looking white, you can't just leave it as it is. You have to keep painting that fence over and over again to keep it looking the same." Building on this, Steve Lemke, Provost of New Orleans Baptist Theological Seminary declares,

> *If we are going to keep Southern Baptists believing that the Bible is the inerrant, infallible Word of God, we're going to have to keep repainting that fence in every generation. We need not only to hold to scriptural authority in our hearts, but to teach it diligently to the next generation, talking to them when we are sitting down, and when we walk in the way, and when we lie down, and when we rise up, and bind them for a sign on our wrists, and as a headband between our eyes, and write them on the mantels of our houses and on our gateposts" (c.f. Deuteronomy 6:4-5).*

---

74   https://www.nobts.edu/faculty/itor/LemkeSW-files/SBCfuture.pdf/ Accessed March 23, 2021

CHAPTER 5

THE CULTURE THAT CHANGED THE CHURCH

WHEREAS THE NEW TESTAMENT CHALLENGES the church to be a transformative agent in this world, some churches appear to have done more conforming than transforming; and sometimes there seems to be a greater push for relevance than righteousness. The church is to be distinctively different from any other organization or community on this earth. One of Southern Baptists most admired statesman, Adrian Rogers, declared, "The church is to stand out in this dark world like a diamond in a coal mine." Southern Baptists would like to think that their Convention would also have that kind of distinctiveness and stand out among other denominations as the leader in theological integrity, moral uprightness and evangelistic fervor. However, there are some who feel that Southern

Baptists are "romancing the world." Ryan Denton of Christ in the Wild Ministries, explained,

> *"As a former SBC Pastor and graduate of an SBC seminary, I'm very concerned with the direction of the SBC. A lot of people and churches are leaving the SBC because of their laxity when it comes to theological commitment and a desire to be set apart from the world."*[75]

THE GREAT EVANGELICAL DISASTER

In the Sermon on the Mount, Jesus urged His disciples to be "salt and light". As salt is meant to arrest the corruption of decaying meat, the church is supposed to arrest the corruption of a decaying society; and as light is meant to dispel the darkness of night, the church is meant to expose and banish the darkness of a perverted society. Unfortunately, it is becoming increasingly evident that the culture is changing the church to a greater extent than the church is changing the culture. The late Francis Schaeffer called the church's conformity to the culture "the great evangelical disaster."

Jesus knew that conforming to the world would be a great temptation for His followers in every age. In His great high priestly prayer, found in John 17, Jesus prayed for His disciples and us: "I do not pray that you should take them out of the world, but that you should keep them from the evil one. They are not of the world, just as I am not of the world." When

---

75   https://christiannews.net/2019/06/11/top-southern-baptist-leaders-take-stage-to-sing-lynyrd-skynyrd-before-thousands-of-pastors-at-send-luncheon/Accessed March 23, 2021

Peter preached his anointed sermon on the Day of Pentecost, he warned his audience and pled with them, "Be saved from this perverse generation" (Acts 2:40). The Apostle Paul rose to the heights of inspired penmanship when he wrote the church in Rome and stated, "I beseech you therefore, brethren, by the mercies of God, that you present your bodies a living sacrifice, holy, acceptable to God, which is your reasonable service. And do not be conformed to this world, but be transformed by the renewing of your mind, that you may prove what is that good and acceptable and perfect will of God" (Romans 12:1-2). James, the half-brother of Jesus, made this same point succinctly and powerfully when he wrote, "Adulterers and adulteresses! Do you not know that friendship with the world is enmity with God? Whoever therefore wants to be a friend of the world makes himself an enemy of God" (James 4:4).

As you can see, the Word of God makes it abundantly clear that the church is to be sanctified and set apart from the world, so that we can effectively change the culture around us. However, in this era of declining church membership and the church's apparent concession with the world, is the church actually changing the culture or is the culture changing the church?

SATAN NEVER STOPS

Satan continues to be feverishly at work to emasculate the church and the people of God. He desperately wants those who have identified with the church to be conformed to his system of thinking rather than transformed by the Word of God. And the devil is so cunning and crafty that most people in the church are not even aware of the suggestive influences that steal into their mind. There is sufficient evidence that many people in our churches, who claim that God's Word is their guidebook for life, have unknowingly embraced worldly ideologies that have had a greater influence upon their thoughts and actions than they realize. It is possible for us to go to church and sing "Victory in Jesus" and not realize there is a battle going on in our lives. Satan wants to capture our mind, because he knows our mind will control our heart and life. That is why Paul wrote to the church at Corinth: "For the weapons of our warfare are not carnal but mighty in God for pulling down strongholds, casting down arguments and every high thing that exalts itself against the knowledge of God, bringing every thought into captivity to the obedience of Christ" (II Corinthians 10:4-5).

We must not let the Master of Deceit have the slightest control over our minds. He wants to inspire our doubting, pervert our doctrine, control our flesh and corrupt our thinking. Daily we should pray the prayer of the Psalmist: "Search me, O God, and know my heart; Try me, and know my anxieties; And see if there is any wicked way in me, And lead me in the way everlasting" (Psalm 139:23-24). We must see that our minds are purged of all that would cripple our Christianity; and then we must occupy the heart, mind and soul so fully with the things of Christ that there can be no room for evil. As members of the body of Christ we must play no part in conforming to this world.

D. L. MOODY'S SERMON ON THE SABBATH

Several years ago, I preached a series of sermons on the Ten Commandments; and prior to preaching those sermons I read Weighed and Wanting a book of sermons on the Decalogue by D. L. Moody, the anointed evangelist who made a great impact for the Lord in both America and Europe, and who died just a few days before the dawning of the 20th century. I was fascinated by the great evangelist's sermons and none impressed me more than his message on the fourth commandment about keeping the Sabbath holy. Working from the point of view that Sunday became a type of Christian Sabbath, Moody declared that there were three great temptations that led people to desecrate the Lord's Day. First, he mentioned the automobile as a deterrent to keeping the Lord's Day, because it provided families the opportunity to take forays into the countryside and away from church services. Although automobiles were introduced in different parts of the United States in the late 1880s, they were mostly rejected due to the high costs. So, I can't really imagine that being a great problem, but Moody identified it as a serious threat to observing the Sabbath. Second, Moody mentioned the bicycle and the excursions it afforded as an impediment to honoring the fourth commandment.

While he spoke of the automobile and the bicycle, the famed evangelist made much of the third temptation he had observed that hindered the faithful worship of God on the Sabbath – the Sunday newspaper.

Moody explained,

With regard to the Sunday newspapers . . . their contents make them unfit for reading any day, not [just]

Sunday. New York dailies advertise Sunday editions of sixty pages. Many dirty pieces of scandal in this and other countries are raked up and put into them. 'Eight pages of fun!' – that is splendid reading for Sunday, isn't it? Even when a so-called sermon is printed, it is completely buried by the fiction and news matter. It is time ministers preached against Sunday newspapers if they haven't done it already.Put the man on the scales that buys and reads Sunday papers. After reading them for two or three hours he might go and hear the best sermon in the world, but you couldn't preach anything into him. His mind is filled up with what he has read, and there is no room for thoughts of God. I believe that the archangel Gabriel himself could not make an impression on an audience that has its head full of such reading. If you bored a hole into a man's head, you could not inject any thoughts of God and heaven. . . Ladies buy the Sunday papers and read the advertisements of Monday bargains to see what they can buy cheap. . .I never read a Sunday paper, and wouldn't have one in my house. . . They do more harm to religion than many other agencies I know. Their whole influence is against keep the Sabbath holy. They are an unnecessary evil.[76]

I share this with you not because I am opposed to Sunday newspapers (perhaps I should be), but to illustrate two things: First, I think it shows us how insensitive we have become to that which militates against a holy life. Is there a preacher who would even consider preaching against Sunday newspapers today? In the 21st century faithful preachers must address catastrophic issues like mob violence, pornography, sex trafficking and pedophilia. Perhaps we are having

---

76   D. L. Moody, Weighed and Wanting, (Moody Press, Chicago) p. 59-62

to deal with these issues because we did not deal with the root of those issues years ago – issues like Sunday newspapers that made idols of Hollywood movie stars and television programming that produced things like scandalous soap operas. Temptations to conform to the world slither into our homes in the most surreptitious and seductive ways.

Moody's denigration of Sunday newspapers illustrates that we can fill our minds with so much cerebral junk food that we squeeze God out of our thinking. And if D. L. Moody was so concerned about the Sunday newspaper having a negative influence on the church of his day, how much more should we be concerned about listening to false teachers, reading ungodly tabloids and spending excessive time on mind-numbing media devices. Satan is using a myriad of cleverly disguised temptations to flood our brains with worldly images, vain philosophies and alternatives to the truth of God.

If Moody drew the line between the use of automobiles, bicycles and newspapers on Sunday and the importance of focusing on spiritual things, like worshipping God in spirit and truth, where should we be drawing the line between the world and the church today. Either Moody was a fool for being so unrealistic and restrictive about the fourth commandment or we have so conformed to the world that we have lost sight of what it means to be holy. Incidentally, I have no intention of calling D. L. Moody a fool; and I am also confessing that at times I have conformed to the world.

Moody was concerned that Christians who read the Sunday newspaper diluted the meaning and effectiveness of their worship experience when they got to church on the Lord's Day. Are there any of our churches today that apply biblical standards to such things as Sunday newspapers, pointless novels, salacious magazines, the violent and suggestive television shows and movies being produced today, and perhaps even more importantly, the harmful impact of the internet on human behavior.

THE LAMP OF THE BODY IS THE EYE

On May 9, 1961 Federal Communications Commission Chairman Newton N. Minow gave a speech before a meeting of television executives and characterized television programming as a "vast wasteland of senseless violence, mindless comedy and offensive advertising."[77] If that was true 60 years ago, how would we describe television programming today? The wasteland is worse than ever, and it includes not only television, but practically every other means of communication available. Have we turned a blind eye to the encroachment of the world into the church? It appears that we have quietly acquiesced and in some cases the culture has influenced the church more than the church has influenced the world.

The Psalmist wrote, "I will behave wisely in a perfect way, Oh, when will You come to me? I will walk within my house with a perfect heart. I will set nothing wicked before my eyes" (Psalm 101:2-3). He is saying that if God visited his home, he would not be ashamed of anything the Lord would see in his heart or in his home. Jesus said, "The lamp of the body is the eye. If therefore your eye is good your whole body will be full of light. But if your eye is bad, your whole body will be full of darkness" (Matthew 6:22-23a). Our eyes are the entrance to our hearts and minds and, as such, they provide

---

77 https://www.history.com/topics/1960s/the-vast-wasteland-of-tele-vision-video(page not found)

a doorway to our very souls. If our eyes focus on godly things, that will radiate outward from within our hearts and minds. If we allow our eyes to linger on evil, the darkness of that evil will begin to emanate from within and can corrupt us and those around us.

The devil knows that he cannot typically get people to choose evil and darkness at the beginning of his temptations, so he will muddle or distort the view of what is good and what is evil in order to dupe us. John Phillips, in his commentary on Matthew, mentioned his problem with astigmatism. Astigmatism causes one's vision to be blurred. Jesus seems to be explaining that it is possible to have spiritual astigmatism – not to have things clearly in focus in our spiritual vision. However, we must never allow the lines between the church and the world to get blurred. There must be a distinctiveness, a uniqueness about the church and the people of God.[78]

The human brain is an incredible organ and has a great capacity for information, but what we put into our brain and what we allow to be put into our brain by others is critical to who we are, what we believe and how we live. When Satan tempted Eve in the Garden of Eden, he promised her that she would become as God, knowing good from evil, if she ate of the fruit from the forbidden tree. It is likely that Eve believed that by eating the fruit she could gain wisdom apart from the wisdom God had given her. Therefore, the temptation was a desire for wisdom apart from God and an independence from God. Today, Satan wants to give us a mindset that is apart from God and a false sense of freedom that will cause us to conform to this world.

---

78   John Phillips, Exploring the Gospel of Matthew, (Kregel Publications, Grand Rapids, Michigan, 2005), p. 118-119

HAPPINESS OVER HOLINESS

In the previous chapter we mentioned that some churches appear to be set on wooing people into their fellowship as satisfied customers. Therefore, they must conclude that if you extract some poor sinner out of the world and put him into a church that preaches the whole counsel of God it is like jerking someone through a knothole. So, in their effort to make their church a welcoming, non-threatening experience they emphasize comfort over commitment and happiness over holiness. I don't know how many Southern Baptist Churches have adopted that philosophy, but it is prevalent in many mainline denominations across America, and we must not allow churches less committed to the sufficiency of Scripture influence our SBC churches to attenuate the Word of God by their emphasis upon methodologies and philosophies that that do not conform to God's truth.

In his blog. Michael Brown writes,

> I have often said the contrast between the contemporary American gospel and the biblical Gospel is this: The contemporary version says, 'This is who I am. This is how I feel. And God is here to please me.' The biblical version says, 'This is who God is. This is how He feels. And I am here to please God.' Consequently, in our modern version of the Gospel, 'sin' is defined as anything that hurts me or makes me uncomfortable. In the biblical version, 'sin' is defined as anything that grieves the Lord or is contrary to His nature."[79]

79 https://www.theclarionsound.com/discipleship/dangerous-trends-
-churches-promoting-self-happiness-over-gods-holiness/Accessed
March 23, 2021

One view is man-centered, the other God-centered. The difference between the two concepts is enormous. Without exaggeration, it is the difference between life and death, salvation and sin, and holiness and happiness. When David sinned, he confessed that his sins haunted him day and night (Psalm 51:3), that he felt dirty (Psalm 51:2), and that he ached as if his bones were broken (Psalm 51:8). His pursuit of his fleshly desires and his venture off into the world did not bring him happiness. In fact, he cried out to God, "Restore unto me the joy of Your salvation" (Psalm 51: 12). Peter on the other hand is the one who gave his great confession of Christ (Matthew 16:16) witnessed the transfiguration (Luke 9:28-36), and preached that great sermon at Pentecost when 3,000 souls were saved (Acts 2:41) and wrote about knowing "joy inexpressible and full of glory" (I Peter 1:8)

God wants you to be happy, but He wants you to be holy more than He wants you to be happy. You will never be happy when you sin, ignore God's will and break His commandments. In fact, when you do that you are headed for destruction. The happiest people on earth are those who believe what God says and faithfully follow Him, regardless of their feelings. We must never conform to this world nor offer the world's happiness to woo people into our churches, because the world's happiness depends on circumstances and is fleeting and temporary. We must lift high the standard of holiness, because that is God's desire for us. He said, "Be ye holy, for I am holy" (I Peter 1:16). Churches that do not hold up that standard have very likely conformed to the world.

THE WORLD HAS INFLUENCED OUR WORSHIP

Some would say that churches that have gone contemporary with dark auditoriums that look like concert halls and performance driven music accented with strobe lights, theatrical fog and resembling a rock band have totally conformed to the world's genre of music, but I am not willing to give a wholesale condemnation of contemporary Christian music for several reasons. First, I know some contemporary Christian artists and I believe their faith and commitment to Christ is as sincere as any servent of God I know. Second, there are pastors and praise band members who embrace contemporary Christian music who are probably as genuine in their walk with Christ as Fannie Crosby, B.B McKinney or Bill Gaither. Third, while I prefer traditional music in my worship experience I am not opposed to contemporary Christian music, because I see how it blesses my children and grandchildren, and I see their Christian commitment and growth in faith.

However, I do not believe any genre of Christian music should try to emulate the music of this world just because it is popular. Careful attention should be given to the words of our songs of praise so that they are absolutely in harmony with Holy Scripture. Furthermore, I believe the symbols of our faith should be honored and preserved. For example, I appreciate those churches that have a pulpit in the center of the platform, because preaching, not music, must be the principal part of the worship experience.

Nevertheless, let me share with you an apprehension about church music that should be a concern to all of us. When I was in seminary, I had a professor of church music who told our class that too many of our hymns are subjective. He claimed that those hymns were man-focused rather than God-focused. He voiced his approval of hymns like "Holy, Holy, Holy", "Praise to the Lord, the Almighty" and "O Worship the King", because those hymns prompted us to direct our attention toward God, our Creator, Sustainer and Redeemer. However, he cautioned us about what he called subjective hymns like "Since Jesus Came into My Heart", "On Jordan's Stormy Banks I Stand", and "Make Me a Blessing." He said those hymns are far too subjective and place the attention on the worshipper rather than the Savior. That sounded good in many ways, because I knew that in our worship God must be the center of our attention and the recipient of our affection. However, at the same time I recognized the need for both kinds of hymns.

Today, I am of the opinion that over a period of years the music of the contemporary church has become almost entirely objective; and that may be a problem. While our focus in worship must be upon God, we must not become so objective and detached from our own sinfulness that we fail to see ourselves as we really are. There are times when we need to sing, "Would He devote that sacred head for sinners such as I?" and "I was sinking deep in sin, far from the peaceful shore" and "I lay my sins on Jesus, the spotless Lamb of God."

When Isaiah went into the temple and saw the Lord high and lifted up, the sight of God's holiness immediately caused Isaiah to recognize his own sinfulness, causing him to cry out, "Woe is me, for I am undone! Because I am a man of unclean lips, and I dwell in the midst of a people of unclean lips; for my eyes have seen the King, the Lord of hosts" (Isaiah 6:5) It was an objective worship experience that brought Isaiah to his knees. But we seem to forget that in chapter 5 Isaiah sang a song that was very subjective about the spiritual condition of his homeland - Judah. I believe it was that song of confession that paved the way for him to see God in his majesty and holiness. Consequently, his life was changed.

Now, if we were to combine the lack of confessional songs in our worship to the lack of confessional prayers in our worship, we have essentially created an environment that makes it difficult for the preacher to declare the whole counsel of God – particularly dealing with issues like personal sins, the need for confession and repentance, judgment and hell. The objective praise songs and the objective prayers of adoration and thanksgiving make the pastor look like a bearer of bad news if he preaches on Colossians 3:5-6 or Galatians 5:19-21 or other passages that communicate that "the wages of sin is death."

When have you heard your pastor pray a confessional prayer in church and ask God to reveal the sins of commission, omission and disposition and bring Holy Ghost conviction upon the congregation? In recent years I have also seldom heard prayers of confession from the pulpits of our churches. In days gone by churches would have bulletins with orders of worship and there would be in the worship agenda, a prayer of invocation, a pastoral prayer, a prayer of confession, an offertory prayer and a benediction. I recently read a book of sermons by George W. Truett, the pastor of the First Baptist Church in Dallas, Texas prior to the ministry of W. A. Criswell, and Truett's prayers are included in the book. He preached a sermon on "The Deadly Danger of Drifting" and prayed,

> *O, we pray that the drifting Christian, no matter what caused the drifting, nor how and where it began, may such Christian this day come back and walk humbly with Christ, and be saved from those burning memories, and those accusations of conscience, which ever*

follow waste and drifting in the Christian life. And still more do we pray, Lord Jesus, that the soul in this place that is going down life's stream, without hope and without God, not saved, not ready to live, not ready to die, not ready for any world, all wrong with God, wrong with the moral universe, wrong with time, wrong with eternity, wrong with earth, wrong with heaven, wrong in every right respect,. . . . wrong in the chiefest way – may such man or women now be helped of God's grace to say: 'As for me this day, God help me, my life is going to be linked with the will of Christ.'"[80]

When there are no confessional songs and confessional prayers in worship service, are we in denial about sin? If we go light on sin in our songs and prayers will that lead to feel good sermons that tend to boost self-esteem.

Years ago, Karl Menninger, a medical professional, wrote a book entitled, "Whatever Became of Sin?" In the book he wrote,

The word 'sin,' which seems to have disappeared, . . . was once a strong word, an ominous and serious word. It described a central point in every civilized human being's life plan and lifestyle. But the word went away. It has almost disappeared – the word, along with the notion. Why? Doesn't anyone sin anymore? Doesn't anyone believe in sin?"[81]

---

80   George W. Truett, A Quest for Souls, (William B. Eerdmans Publishing Company, Grand Rapids, Michigan, 1963) p. 180

81   Karl Menninger, Whatever Became of Sin? (Hawthorn Books, New York, 1973) p. 14

Menninger expressed concern that the loss of a sin consciousness did not stop as a trend in secular culture. It also became popular in mainstream evangelicalism to the extent that a serious consideration of sin in many circles of the church has become unthinkable. Is it possible that we are becoming like the people in Jeremiah's day when he asked the question, "Are they ashamed of their detestable conduct?" He answers his own question when he replied, "No! They were not at all ashamed, Nor did they know how to blush" (Jeremiah 8:12 NIV). If, indeed, we have, even though perhaps unknowingly, allowed our prayers, songs and perhaps even our preaching to become void of the sinfulness of man and the need for repentance? Perhaps, in order to gain a sense of security, albeit false, we have allowed the proverbial camel to slip his nose under the tent.Is our lack of focus on sin and the confession of sin not an indication of conformity to the world?

SOUTHERN BAPTISTS' VIEW ON ALCOHOL

There is some evidence that Southern Baptists have succumbed to some of the world's standards. At the Southern Baptist Convention in Greensboro, North Carolina in 2006 a resolution was presented to the messengers "On Alcohol Use in America." One of the stated reasons for the resolution was that there are "some religious leaders who are now advocating the consumption of alcoholic beverages based on a misinterpretation of the doctrine of 'our freedom in Christ.'" I was on the resolutions committee that year and was amazed at the lengthy floor debate when the resolution was presented to the messengers. There were pastors who spoke against the resolution. Baptist Press stated that the resolution was adopted by an 80 percent majority. There were 11,639 messengers at the Southern Baptist Convention annual session in 2006. If Baptist Press' estimate was correct there could have been as many as 2,327 Southern Baptists, many of whom were pastors and church staff members, who opposed the resolution. Compare that to the 1896 Southern Baptist Convention that officially denounced alcohol and asked that churches excommunicate anyone who sold or drank alcohol. [See Appendix A for both the 2006 and 1896 resolutions]

There was a time when many Baptist churches had a church covenant. This covenant included the church members' promise "to abstain from the sale of and use of intoxicating drinks as a beverage." Those covenants were often glued to the inside cover of our hymnals. Larger versions of the covenant were placed on the wall of the church in a strategic place. In the last few decades, I have only occasionally seen one of those covenants in our churches, but apparently the covenant has gone the way of the hymnals. Check the internet and you will find multiple articles indicating that "Beer is Americas' adult beverage of choice". The fact that a significant percentage of Southern Baptists may have grown soft on drinking is troubling, but perhaps more than anything else it is just symbolic of the church being conformed to the world. [See Appendix B to read the church covenant in full]

COMPLEMENTARIANS VS. EGALITARIANS

In recent years Southern Baptists have had numerous debates over the complementarian/egalitarian issue. The complementarian view, which Southern Baptists have historically embraced, is the view that men and women are of equal intrinsic value but have different functioning roles in the church. This view rejects the ordination of women as pastors or deacons and does not support the idea of women preaching. The egalitarian view avows that women are equal to men in terms of their rights and responsibilities in the church and can exercise spiritual authority as clergy.

As we have previously mentioned, a resolution was adopted by 58 percent of the messengers at the 1984 convention in Kansas City, stating that "women are not in public worship to assume a role of authority over men lest confusion reign in the local church".

The 2000 Baptist Faith and Message also espouses the complementarian view. Section VI of the BF&M pertains to "The Church" and states: "Its (the church's) spiritual officers are pastors and deacons. While both men and women are gifted for service in the church, the office of pastor is limited to men as qualified by Scripture". However, the sentiment for a move toward an egalitarian philosophy surfaces periodically; and it appears that there has been considerable discussion in recent years to once again elevate the status of women in the SBC.

Southern Baptists may have thought that the Convention's adherence to a complementarian position on the role of women was unalterable, but a "tweet" from Beth Moore, one of America's most notable Bible teachers, rekindled the fires of enthusiasm for those who were of a more egalitarian mindset. Moore tweeted, "You may not support a woman teaching from the platform, but you cannot use Scripture to claim women did not and cannot in any way lead. If women in crisis never see women in visible roles in church and never hear from them, what on earth would ever make them think they would be heard." Moore was criticized for her comment, but

Wade Burleson, lead pastor of Emmanuel Baptist Church in Enid, Oklahoma, defended her by saying, "Beth does Christian ministry. She shouldn't need to defend her ministry to Southern Baptist Caucasian males who've fallen into the doctrinal trap of the eternal subordination of women."[82]

While some few Southern Baptist Churches may ordain women for pastoral roles, the SBC typically does not, but it is of some concern that the discussion has been on the table recently. Practically all of the evangelical churches in America are now ordaining women. The United Methodist Church in America has granted ordination and full clergy rights to women since 1956; and twenty-one of them have been elevated to the episcopacy. Almost ten years ago Dr. Chuck Kelley, who was then president of New Orleans Baptist Theological Seminary, wrote a paper entitled, *Southern Baptists are the New Methodists.* Will Southern Baptists conform to the current evangelical culture and follow the course of the United Methodists by ordaining women in the coming years? While the culture may encourage it, the Word of God forbids it.

CAN TRUSTEES BE TRUSTED?

If you were the leader of some organization that was structured to have trustees with the fiduciary responsibilities of making decisions in the best interests of its constituents and to whom you were accountable, you would probably try to ingratiate yourself to those trustees by any legitimate

---

82   https://www.washingtonpost.com/religion/2019/06/09/southern-baptists-are-supposed-talk-about-sex-abuse-right-now-theyre-discussing-whether-one-woman-can-preach/Accessed March 23, 2021

means available. You would want them to be your friends and approve of your leadership and vote to support your vision for the institution or agency you had been called to direct. However, trustees of businesses and corporations are compelled do all they can to protect the best interests of their shareholders; and the trustees of SBC entities are primarily accountable, not to the leaders of their agencies, but to the Baptists in the pews of our churches, many of whom sacrifice to support their agencies, and they are ultimately accountable to God. It is a matter of Christian stewardship for Baptist trustees to accept their roles not as a status symbol or an honor to be coveted, but as a sacred responsibility.

The trustees of our institutions and agencies are responsible for approving budgets and accounting for how money is spent. With trustees holding such power over assets on behalf of millions of Baptists, our Father in heaven and the laws of the land impose on them a fiduciary duty to be impartial and faithful stewards. In recent years concerned Baptists have asked multiple questions about the Ethics and Religious Liberty Commission, and the North American Mission Board as well as certain seminaries. When suspicions, questions and doubts about an agency begin to surface, trustees need to act quickly to make sure they don't lose their integrity, the ability to right the ship (agency), or forfeit the right to ask Southern Baptists to continue their financial support.

That must have happened in the dustup between the LifeWay trustees and the agency's former president, Thom Ranier. According to several news sources, including The Baptist Message, the state publication for the Louisiana Baptist Convention, when Ranier retired he received a transitional salary of more than $1 million, plus benefits, not including royalty payments on his books published by LifeWay. He also signed a non-compete clause that was to continue until October, 2021.

The LifeWay trustees stated that the vast majority were unaware of the lucrative deal that had been made with Ranier. When the former LifeWay president violated the terms of his severance agreement and signed a book contract with Tyndale House Publishers, a LifeWay competitor, some of the trustees moved to action by issuing a lawsuit against Ranier. Board member and former chairman of the LifeWay trustees Jimmy Scroggins, led a campaign to withdraw the lawsuit claiming, "Lawsuits between believers are public, embarrassing, and damaging to the kingdom." Within a week the issue was satisfactorily settled without any legal action being necessary. The trustees' action may have quickly prompted a solution to the issue, but it is a method the Bible does not endorse. I Corinthians 6:1-11 tells us that there are better ways to handle disputes among believers. When the LifeWay trustees resorted to a lawsuit, they emulated or conformed to the way of the world.

Dr. Christopher Bart Barber, pastor of First Baptist Church of Farmersville, Texas, in his booklet Why Southern Baptists Need the Trustee System asserts, "The greatest commendation for the trustee-board system is the fact that it has facilitated so much good work for the kingdom of God on such a large scale for so long with so little trouble (comparatively)." But he also adds,

> *The objections of critics (of the trustee system) are not altogether without merit. Southern Baptists have endured seasons of wasteful bureaucracy, criminal malfeasance, executive ineptitude and theological heterodoxy in our 162 years of existence. Each episode has amounted to a failure of the Southern Baptist structure of trustee oversight.*[83]

---

83   https://www.yumpu.com/en/document/read/45863179/why-sou-

Randy Adams, the Executive Director-Treasurer of the Northwest Baptist Convention, in a press release in early 2021 expressed grave concern over a number of issues in the Southern Baptist Convention and summed it up by writing:

The most precious commodities of the SBC mission's system are trust and goodwill. These have been eroded significantly, but through transparency and accountable leadership they can be rebuilt. Indeed, they must be rebuilt if we are to preserve and grow the miraculous missionary system we inherited from our forefathers. We need to reform the system, crush corruption, and rebuild trust in our cooperative missionary endeavor.

If trust and goodwill have eroded, if the system needs to be reformed, if corruption must be crushed and if trust needs to be rebuilt in our institutions and agencies something is terribly wrong and makes Southern Baptists look very much like the world. So, how can salt arrest the corruption in the world if the salt has lost its savor?

---

thern-baptists-need-the-trustee-system-baptist-theology/Accessed March 23, 2021

CHAPTER 6 ➡

HAS EVANGELISM GONE WITH THE WIND?

ANYONE LIVING IN THE ATLANTA area almost has to know all about Margaret Mitchell and her novel, *Gone with the Wind*. The book, first published in 1936, portrays Mitchell's concept of what life was like in the South following the American Civil War and Reconstruction era. The story is set in Atlanta and Clayton County just south of Georgia's capital city. The story focuses on Scarlett O'Hara, the indulged daughter of a wealthy plantation owner who struggles to pick up the pieces of a shattered life after General Sherman's devastating march through the state to Savannah on the coast. The title of the book is derived from Scarlett O'Hara's statement when she wonders to herself if her plantation home, called Tara, is still standing or if it is "gone with the wind" – a reference to Sherman's tornadic march through Georgia.

FORGIVE THE REMINISCENCE

When certain people look at our beloved convention today, they see a Christian body in decline and wonder if the once growing, influential Southern Baptist Convention is "gone with the wind." For decades, Southern Baptists have been known for evangelistic fervor and missionary zeal. Those of us who have been around for eight decades remember two-week long revival meetings and two-week Vacation Bible Schools and pastors urging their congregations to regularly share "the Roman Road" plan of salvation with those who were lost. I remember that there were 26 individuals baptized on the Sunday night I was baptized in a First Baptist church in a small town in Western North Carolina. I remember when practically all of the sermons were evangelistic in nature and that passionate, pleading invitations were given. It was more commonplace than occasional to sing through "Just As I Am" or "Pass Me Not, Oh Gentle Savior" several times as the invitation to Christ continued..

I remember when state convention evangelism departments promoted simultaneous revivals in one section of the state after another.

I remember when Ed and Bette Stalnecker along with hundreds of Southern Baptist Evangelists sent out universal invitations to messengers from every corner and clime of the nation to come to their fellowship after the Southern Baptist Convention concluded its Wednesday evening session. Music evangelists sang heartwarming music. Preaching evangelists gave testimonies of God moving in the revivals and evangelistic crusades they had conducted. There was hardly room enough in the largest reserved ballroom in the convention hotel for everyone who wanted to attend the inspiring gathering.

For many years, the Home Mission Board (now the North American Mission Board) had dozens if not scores of personnel in their Evangelism Department to promote soul winning. Volumes of material was published to help churches equip their membership in personal soul winning and to assist them in establishing effective outreach programs. State evangelism conferences were characterized with rousing music and powerful preaching that inspired attendees to go back to their churches as impassioned witnesses for Christ. The pastors who attended the conferences returned to their pulpits with a fire burning in their hearts to preach the Gospel without fear or favor; and many of them had a renewed desire to see their people mobilized to reach the lost at any cost.

Because of the emphasis placed on evangelism in our convention I was always trying to find new and effective ways to train our church members to become personal soul winners. In my first church I taught our deacons to use the afore mentioned Roman Road to explain God's plan of salvation. We just simply used passages of scripture from Paul's Epistle to the Romans to explain how those who were unredeemed could become a part of God's forever family. Then there was a period when I used Billy Graham's "Steps to Peace with God" as our evangelism tool - later it was Campus Crusade's (Cru's) "Four Spiritual Laws" then "Evangelism Explosion." When Southern Baptists came out with Continuing Witness Training" (CWT) I drove from Jackson, Mississippi for a training session at First Baptist Church Lilburn, Georgia, where Howard Ramsey taught the class for pastors all across the southeast. At Eastside we trained almost 300 people to use F.A.I.T.H. Evangelism, a soul winning model developed by Bobby Welch, former SBC President, who during his two-year tenure as the elected leader of our convention traveled to all 50 states promoting evangelism and personal soul winning. I had the privilege of going witnessing with him on his stop at Richmond Hills Baptist Church near Savannah.

Southern Baptists became the largest non-Catholic denomination in America because there was a passion to reach the lost and baptize those who were saved into the fellowship of the local church. I suppose it was in the 1950s that Convention Press published a study course book entitled "One to Eight." The primary emphasis of the book was to get the "baptism – church member" ratio down to one person baptized in a year for every eight church members. I do not remember the exact ratio during that time period, but it was probably one to twelve or close to that. In 2019 Southern Baptists baptized one person for every 62 members. Obviously, we have more money, finer facilities, larger church staffs, greater means of communicating the Gospel and a much larger pool of lost people, but we are reaching fewer people.

THE GREAT COMMISSION RESURGENCE TASK FORCE

I greatly fear that when the Great Commission Resurgence Task Force presented their recommendations to the SBC annual meeting in Orlando, Florida in June 2010 there was a fatal flaw in the report. Component Four of the report pertained to reaching North America and included these words:

> *The North American Mission Board must be refocused and unleashed for greater effectiveness. Therefore, we call upon Southern Baptists to affirm NAMB with a priority to plant churches in North America, reach our cities and underserved regions and people groups, and clarify its*

role to lead and accomplish efforts to reach North America with the Gospel. . . We desire for the North American Mission Board to encourage Southern Baptist churches to become church planting congregations.

The report also specified that 50-percent of the ministry efforts of the North American Board be given to assist churches in planting healthy, multiplying and faithful Baptist congregations in the U. S. and Canada.[84]

In February 2021 NAMB announced that they were allocating $5 million to support student-focused evangelism outreach across North America over the next four years. Baptist Press reported-

This decision was made because statistics show that Southern Baptists baptized 38 percent fewer teenagers last year than in 2000. A 2018 Barna study revealed that 42 percent of the Gen Z generation (those born between 1999 and 2015) say they identify with a faith besides Christianity or have no faith at all. Additionally, a 2019 Barna study indicated that nearly half of Christian millennials (those born between 1984 and 1998) declared it wrong to share their faith with the goal of seeing another person come to Christ.[85]

While the NAMB budget allocation to reach students is certainly a step in the right direction, $1.25 million a year

---

84 Penetrating the Lostness: Embracing a Vision for a Great Commission Resurgence Among Southern Baptists, p. 4

85 https://www.baptistpress.com/resource-library/news/namb-ec-announce-5-million-boost-for-student-evangelism-efforts/Accessed March 23, 2021

represents less than one percent of the entity's budget. However, the agency is also going to distribute $4.5 million in evangelism grant funds to non-South state conventions.

Dr. Chuck Kelley, former president of New Orleans Baptist Theological Seminary, states in his book, *The Dilemma of Decline,*

> *The decade since GCR was adopted in 2010 has not been good for the Southern Baptist Convention. What was intended to be a Great Commission Resurgence driven by a radical new direction from NAMB in fact became a Great Commission Regression, adding to the decline that began in 2000 rather than reversing it, with losses unprecedented in SBC history.*[86]

While I am certain the Task Force was highly motivated to craft a worthy plan for reaching North America with the Gospel and believed that a reinvention of the North American Mission Board was in order, I fear that they may not have taken into consideration one incontrovertible truth: evangelism is how you build the church. To attempt to start a church before you evangelize is like building the penthouse of a skyscraper before you lay the foundation.

Before the church was organized and functioning as the body of Christ, there was a lot of preaching and evangelistic work that was necessary. The 120 disciples who were filled with the Holy Spirit spoke to all those who had come to Jerusalem about the "wonderful works of God" (Acts 2:6-11). Peter preached on the Day of Pentecost, souls were saved (Acts 2:14-39) and then the church was developed. When Paul went

---

86   Charles S. Kelley Jr., The Dilemma of Decline: Southern Baptists Face a New Reality, Colter & Co., Dallas, Texas, 2020) p. 47

to Philippi, he witnessed to Lydia and baptized her and her family, cast a demon out of a young woman, led the Philippian jailer to salvation and baptized him and his family. All that took place before any mention of a church in Philippi. When you go into an under-served people group, you don't plant a church and develop an "if we build it, they will come" philosophy. You evangelize the lost in order to plant churches; and that is why evangelism must forever be a priority for any Christian, any church and any convention or denomination.

THE DILEMMA OF DECLINE

As Dr. Kelley points out in *The Dilemma of Decline*, Southern Baptists baptized approximately 257,000 people into their churches in 1945. A decade later, in 1955, they baptized approximately 417,000. In 2019 Southern Baptist Churches baptized 235,748 individuals, the lowest number since World War II. Kelley indicated that from 2011-2018 the SBC lost an average of 1,144 churches a year. These are churches who gave up their Convention ID number. In 2000, the average number of baptisms per SBC church was 9.97. By 2019, the average number of baptisms per church was 4.9, a drop of fifty percent.

In 2019, the SBC membership declined by 287,655 – the greatest loss in 100 years. Interestingly and alarmingly, in the past 15 years the population of the United States has increased by approximately 37.1 million people. During that same period of time Southern Baptist membership declined by almost two million. It is obvious that we are losing the battle for souls.

Incidenttaly, several years ago there was another effort to change the name of the Convention, but ultimately messengers were asked to approve a recommendation to use the unofficial moniker "Great Commission Baptists". However, it is almost hypocritical to be called "Great Commission Baptists". In fact, evangelism has become such an afterthought in Southern Baptist life that at the Southern Baptist Convention's annual meeting in Dallas in 2018, a young pastor from Indiana made a motion that the messengers consider the establishment of an entity that would focus on inspiring and leading SBC churches to reach the lost at all costs. Furthermore, as the population of the nation grows, and the membership of the churches decline, the denomination loses its impact on the nation and the church loses its influence in its local community.

On March 3, 2009, Dr. Kelley addressed the NOBTS family in chapel with a message entitled, *"The New Methodist: Reflections on the SBC Today."* He stated-

I love Methodists! They played a key role in the First and Second Great Awakenings. Their concept of a circuit riding preacher was a brilliant strategy for the circumstances of the day. With it they were able to multiply church starts faster than they multiplied church pastors, enabling them to evangelize the American Frontier in the 19th and early 20th centuries. They made holy living a core value; and were called Methodists because they went about it so systematically and methodically. Much of what Southern Baptists know about evangelistic harvesting we learned from Methodist."

Kelley continued-

> *The Methodists of today, however, have changed much through the years. Their efforts in evangelism and missions have greatly diminished. The passion for holy living has been replaced by behavior blending with the culture. Their greatest theological fight is over the normalcy of homosexuality. Most surprisingly, they have set new records for the fastest loss of membership in the history of the church in America. Having observed these changes in Methodism, I find myself admitting today that we are following in their footsteps. Southern Baptists are the New Methodists.*"[87]

I think there are several reasons why our baptisms are declining and why there is considerable talk about it, but so little action.

A LACK OF COMPASSION FOR THE LOST

First, I wonder sometimes if Christians have all that much of a joyful anticipation of heaven and all that much of a dreadful fear of hell. In other words, many of us may minimize the horrors of hell and rationalize that it is not a bad as it is portrayed in the Bible. There is no urgent, compelling, overwhelming reason to warn people about the wrath to come, because many have padded their nests down here most comfortably and have an extreme earthbound syndrome. We are not like Jesus when he saw the lostness of the people of Jerusalem. In Matthew 9:36 the Bible says, "But when He saw

---

87 https://www.nobts.edu/baptist-center-theology/papers-files/Kelley_New_Methodists.pdf/Accessed March 23, 2021

the multitudes, He was moved with compassion for them, because they were weary, and scattered, like sheep having no shepherd." The Greek word for "moved with compassion" is "splagnitzomai" which means "moved to the point of having an emotional upheaval." This Greek word is used only five times in the Bible, and it is only used of Jesus, because no one ever cared for people like He did. He touched the untouchable, loved the unlovable, taught the unteachable and cared for every barefooted-nobody who ever walked on the earth. He didn't want anyone to go to hell and he would plead and bleed for the salvation of souls.

The Apostle Paul had a similar concern for people. He had an emotional and physical reaction when he went to Athens and saw all the idols and heard all the vain philosophies of the men who debated in the marketplace and the Areopagus. The Bible says, 'His spirit was provoked within him when he saw that the city was given over to idols" (Acts 17:16). Paul was in the city of brilliant men – Pericles, Demosthenes, Socrates, Plato, Aristotle, Sophocles and Euripides, but all their knowledge and sophistication had produced nothing but idolatry. It stirred Paul's heart. It moved him to action. He was a passionate preacher with an indomitable spirit. Neither beatings, shipwreck, deprivation or imprisonment prevented Paul from sharing the Gospel.

David Brainerd had a spiritual obsession to win native American tribes in the northeast to Christ. He was a sickly evangelist who died at age 30, but on July 21, 1744 he wrote these words in his diary-

Towards night my burden respecting my work among the Indians began to increase much. I began to be in anguish. I cared not what or how I lived, or what hardships I went through, so that I could but gain souls for Christ.[88]

Brainerd's quote reminded me of John Knox who prayed, "Give me Scotland or I die." Or of Suzanna Wesley, mother of 19 children including John and Charles Wesley, who prayed, "Oh God, I will not stand before thee without all my children." William Booth, founder of the Salvation Army said, "Some men's ambition is art. Some men's ambition is fame. Some men's ambition is gold. My ambition is the souls of men."[89]

Charles H. Spurgeon, pastor of the Metropolitan Tabernacle in London in the last half of the 19th century, said-

If sinners be damned, at least let them leap into Hell over our dead bodies. And if they perish, let them perish with our arms wrapped about their knees, imploring them to be saved. If Hell must be filled, let it be filled in the teeth of our exertions, and let not one go unwarned and unprayed for."[90]

Those who do not have a clear picture of eternity, the absolute blessedness of heaven and the unmitigated fear of hell will not likely be impassioned soul winners. I fear we have lost our evangelistic passion.

---

88 Penetrating the Lostness: Embracing a Vision for a Great Commission Resurgence Among Southern Baptists, p. 4

89 https://www.family-times.net/illustration/Ambition/200069/Accessed March 23, 2021

90 https://www.goodreads.com/quotes/74181-if-sinners-be-damned-at-least-let-them-leap-to/Accessed March 23, 2021

A RELUCTANCE TO EMBRACE THE EXCLUSIVITY OF THE GOSPEL

Second, those who have questions about the exclusivity of the Gospel basically disqualify themselves as a witness for Christ. Years ago, Josh McDowell, the Christian apologist, said, "Today's generation has replaced John 3:16 - the message of salvation – as the most quoted verse in the Bible with Matthew 7:1, 'Judge not, that you be not judged.'"[91] While this verse was given to teach us to judge according to God's standard as evidenced by His character and nature, it had been construed to mean something the Lord never intended. Our culture has taken this verse to justify developing a doctrine of tolerance that gives credence to all religions. Thus, we live in a day when a growing number of people believe all religions are valid; and those who believe that Jesus is the only way to heaven are considered extremists or bigots.

My wife and I were in Vancouver, British Columbia to board a cruise ship to Alaska and were transported from the airport to our hotel by a taxi driver with a long beard and wearing a turban. He was listening to a CD of Eastern classical music. I asked him about his religious background, and he told me he was a Sikh. I proceeded to talk to him about Jesus, His love for sinners, His miraculous birth, sinless life, atoning death and victorious resurrection. He responded by saying, "I know about Jesus and His life and I believe in all you have said. I believe in all good religions. I believe in doing good

---

91   https://www.baptistpress.com/resource-library/news/te-ens-attracted-to-the-truths-of-christ-through-relationship-s-says-josh-mcdowell/#:~:text=Today's%20generation%2C%20McDowell%20said%2C%20has%20replaced%20John%203%3A16,s-tandard%20as%20evidenced%20by%20his%20character%20and%20nature/Accessed March 23, 2021

works and living a good life and keeping God in my heart all the time."

I continued to try to impress on Him that the only way to have one's sins forgiven and receive the hope of eternal life is through Jesus. I quoted Scripture and gave him my own testimony. Finally, he held up his right hand as we were crossing the bridge over the Burrard Inlet. He said, "Look at the fingers of my hand." He began to hold up one finger after another and said, "This finger represents Sikhism. This finger represents Christianity. This finger represents Islam. This finger represents Buddhism, but as you can see, they all lead to my hand. My hand represents the place where my soul will experience a rebirth after I die."

Our taxi driver was a very friendly, kind gentleman and it would have been very easy to have backed off and congratulated him on his inclusive perspective on religions, but I knew better than to think he was a part of God's family. I tried to lovingly press the uniqueness of Jesus and the inimitability of the Gospel as the only pathway to heaven. He did not pray to receive Christ, but I prayed with him, gave him a Gospel tract and a copy of the Gospel of John. I don't profess to be an exemplary soul winner, but I do know that if you get soft or lukewarm in your commitment to the exclusivity of the Gospel and begin to entertain the thought that all religions lead to the same place you will never be a conscientious witness for Christ.

Sharing the Gospel with an unregenerated society is not an easy task, but it never has been. We must love people of all faiths and we must try to understand the heritage and background of all religions, but we must be committed to the exclusivity of the Gospel of Jesus Christ. If a salesman believes other companies make products equally good or better, he will never be a super salesman.

We live in a pluralistic society, as we have already noted in a previous chapter, and this was succinctly illustrated when Senator Bernie Sanders asked Russell Vought, nominated by President Trump to be deputy director of the Office of Management and Budget about his beliefs. "Do you believe people in the Muslim religion stand condemned?" Sanders repeatedly asked about Muslims, emphasizing that Vought's belief in the exclusivity of the Gospel as Islamophobic. "What about Jews?" Sanders asked, "Do they stand condemned, too? In your judgement, do you think that people who are not Christians are going to be condemned?"

Vought responded, "I am a Christian. I believe all individuals are made in the image of God and are worthy of dignity and respect regardless of their religious beliefs." However, throughout the merciless interrogation Vought continued to emphasize "the centrality of Jesus Christ in salvation." We can appreciate Vought's strong stand for Christ under the pressure of a senate inquiry and in view of recent polls that show about half of all Christians in the U. S. believe that some non-Christians can go to heaven.[92]

Bernie Sander's relentless badgering of Vought is a prime example of the world's opinion that Christians are narrow-minded bigots. Claiming to have a monopoly on the truth may seem prejudicial to most, but those who propose to carry out the Great Commission must risk the abuse and ridicule. It may sound loving and charitable to seek to broaden the narrow road by embracing a philosophy of inclusiveness and universalism, but we must remember that Jesus declared, "I am the way, the truth, and the life. No one comes to the Father except through Me" (John 14:6) One must believe those

---

92   https://www.npr.org/sections/thetwo-way/2017/06/09/532116365/
     is-it-hateful-to-believe-in-hell-bernie-sanders-questions-prompt-
     -backlash/Accessed March 23, 2021

words of Christ, see the world as a mission field and risk ridicule and perhaps even persecution in order to be a zealous and consistent soul winner.

A LACK OF TRAINING

Third, in this age of religious pluralism and vain philosophies a believer must have some knowledge of Christian apologetics or he may feel ill prepared to become a zealous witness. As I am sure you have already determined, I am well on in years and near the finish line of this earthy pilgrimage. I recognize that years and years ago there were fewer distractions and not as many pointless and foolish philosophies to muddle the minds of those who were lost. There was also a greater consciousness of sin, and people were more open to the Gospel. In most cases you could lovingly guide unbelievers down the Roman Road, highlight the steps to salvation and people would understand and often respond to the glorious Gospel and be saved.

Today, as we have already mentioned, many people are so filled with the junk food of this world that it takes a knowledgeable witness to expose all the destructive dogmas and paralyzing ideologies, dispel all the diabolical lies, and answer all the questions of those who will listen to a Gospel witness. The Greek word *apologia* means "defense," such as a lawyer gives in a courtroom trial. Christian apologetics is a defense of the faith; and as believers we must heed the admonition of the Apostle Peter who wrote, "But sanctify the Lord God in your hearts, and always be ready to give a defense to everyone who asks you a reason for the hope that is in you, with meekness and fear" (I Peter 3:15).

Today's witnesses need to be trained and armed with the information necessary to respond to the questions and excuses hurled at them by the lost, and they must be equipped to expose the foolish ideologies of the natural man who does not understand the things of the Spirit of God (See I Corinthians 2:14). I fear that many believers are hesitant to go witnessing because they feel incapable of answering the questions the devil may inspire in the hearts of unregenerate souls.

A FAILURE TO MOBILIZE THE CHURCH TO REACH THE LOST

Fourth, few pastors are mobilizing and equipping an army of soulwinners to fulfill the Great Commission; and there may be nothing more important for a pastor to do than training his church membership to penetrate the darkness of this world with the Gospel. We have already stated that in 2019, the ratio of Southern Baptist church members to baptisms was 62 to 1. In other words, it took 62 Southern Baptists 365 days to win one person to faith in Christ. According to Baptist Press, Southern Baptists church members gave a total amount of approximately $11.6 billion in the offering plates of their churches. If you divide that amount by the number of baptisms, you will discover that it took over $49,200 to win one soul to Christ.

Dr. Chuck Kelley, who has repeatedly addressed the reality of the decline in the SBC, recently wrote that after banging on that drum for more than a decade he had finally gotten a response. He wrote, "The president of the North

American Mission Board and some other SBC leaders finally acknowledge the decline of the SBC and pledged to address it in a video, 'It's on Me.' You can't fix a problem you don't think you have."[93]

The "fix" needs to begin in the local church with pastors setting the pace in soul winning, because church members will seldom do better than the pastor. Pastors who wish to mobilize an army of believers to witness could at least set aside two hours a week, get the chairman of the deacons to accompany him on soulwinning visitation, and do some on-the-job training in the process.

DON'T FAIL TO PREACH FOR A COMMITMENT

Fifth, I fear that many pastors are not preaching passionate sermons for the purpose of getting a response. In his autobiography, *A Life Without Compromise*, Bailey Smith has a chapter entitled, "A Mighty Encounter with the Living God." In this chapter he tells about an experience he had in his small study at home when he was pastor of First Southern Baptist Church in Del City, Oklahoma. He recalled-

All of a sudden there came upon me a sense of a presence in that little office. It was both exciting and fearsome. In that presence a voice spoke to my heart, no not verbally, that changed my life forever. The message from that voice was that I was to preach with a boldness and a power that I had never preached with before. I believe with all my heart God said to me, 'If I tell

---

93   Kelley, Jr., Obit. p. 56

you to say something and you don't say it, it may not get said'. . . .I felt the Lord had come into my presence and told me I must be a strong, uncompromising prophet who would preach to the point of bringing people under conviction."[94]

Of course, Smith's faithfulness to that encounter with God and his effectiveness as a pastor and an evangelist are legendary.

The fiery evangelist continued-

I began to sense that power and I know some of the things I was saying were harsh, but sometimes it takes a loud voice to wake someone up. Sometimes it takes an irritating fire alarm to get someone out of the house and to safety. Most people who go to church today get back in their car after church exactly the way they got out of it. The preacher said nothing that challenged, convicted, or condemned them. There was a day when people came to church to hear a man of God and they walked the aisle confessing their sins. Today they go to church and hear a motivational speaker and never consider their sins."[95]

Dr. Hershael York, Dean of the School of Theology at Southern Baptist Theological Seminary, stated-

The prophets, the apostles and Jesus never had to choose between biblical fidelity and passionate preaching. Stephen would never have been stoned or James killed

---

94   Bailey Smith, A Life Without Compromise, p.122.

95   Ibid. p. 123

with the sword had their preaching been dull. Farmers, fisherman and housewives would not have stood hours on end in the hot Galilean sun, listening to Jesus preach, if He were reciting the beatitudes the way most preachers read them in the pulpit. Ezekiel, Jeremiah, Amos, Joel, Elijah . . . all preached with such passion that people heard, understood and reacted to their message.

York continued-

Most preaching today would hardly warrant the notice of Satan's crowd, let alone a stoning. Surely, heaven groans when we turn the beautiful Gospel of Jesus Christ into the source of so many yawns."[96]

LAZINESS IS AN IMPEDIMENT TO EVANGELISM

Sixth, many churches may be flagging in their zeal to launch a witnessing ministry simply because it is hard work. Some believers might reject the idea of becoming conversant with the principles of apologetics or object to the need for becoming equipped to refute the ideologies and answer the questions of the unredeemed, but no one has ever said that being a soul-winner is easy. In fact, it is an agonizing, laborious task. The Apostle Paul compared the work of soul-winning to "the travail, the labor pains" a woman experiences in giving birth to a child (Galatians 4:19).

---

96   Jerry Vines and Adam B. Dooley, Passion in the Pulpit (Moody Publishers, Chicago, Illinois, 2018) p. 12

Why is the task of soul-winning so difficult?

(1) Witnessing is not easy **mentally**, because it requires learning how to share the Gospel and equipping oneself to respond to all the questions that an unbeliever might ask.

(2) Witnessing is not easy **physically**, because it requires one to forsake his well-worn recliner and the comforts of home to go out like the faithful postman who once declared, "Neither snow, nor rain, nor heat, nor gloom of night stays (this) courier from the swift completion of (his) appointed rounds."

(3) Witnessing is not easy **emotionally**, because it requires not only a spiritual response to the needs of the lost, but a heartfelt response to the condition of the lost.

It is not easy, but we are reminded that the Psalmist said, "Those who sow in tears Shall reap in joy. He who continually goes forth weeping, Bearing seed for sowing, Shall doubtless come again with rejoicing, Bringing his sheaves with him" (Psalm 126: 5-6).

I sat in the den of a lost man one night for whom I had prayed for weeks, with tears streaming down my face, I presented the Gospel to him, and wept even larger crocodile tears at his rejection of my witnessing efforts. When I left him, I was emotionally drained. The next day, he called me and said, "Preacher, I couldn't sleep last night. All I could think of was your tears for me and that if you are that concerned about the condition of my soul, I realize I need to show some concern for myself. Please come back and tell me what I need to do to follow through on what you shared with me."

(4) Witnessing is not easy **spiritually.** When the Apostle Paul penned, "That I may know Him, and the power of His resurrection, and the fellowship of His sufferings, being conformed to His death" (Philippians 3:10), he was talking about sharing the burden, even the sufferings, of the Son of God for a lost world and a growing church. There are three kinds of suffering mentioned in the Bible. First, there is suffering for sin; and we call that punishment. Second, there is suffering for Christ; and we call that persecution. Third, there is suffering with Christ; and we call that passion. George McDonald said, "Jesus did not suffer and die in order to save us from suffering, but that our suffering might be like His."[97] Jesus has told us to take up our cross and follow Him, a command that required obedience, which is a spiritual matter. Junior Hill, a God-sent, heavenly-anointed evangelist, proclaimed, "Jesus also said, 'Follow me and I will make you fishers of men.' And the truth is if you aren't fishing, you aren't following." Those who have been washed in the precious blood of Jesus must do the difficult thing and go into the highways and hedges, the cities and hamlets, the skyscraper condominiums and the humble cottages of our land to declare that "Jesus saves!"

---

97 https://www.preachingtoday.com/illustrations/2004/july/15423.html/Accessed March 23, 2021

I appreciate Dr. Kelley's longing and desire to see Southern Baptists reverse the dangerous decline we are experiencing, and his suggestions for the revitalization of evangelistic fervor. He pleads-

> *(1) Declare the rebirth of evangelism! (Do it) Publicly! (2) Restructure NAMB! NAMB leadership must return to a passionate embrace of the historic SBC assignment to assist churches with evangelism. (3) Focus on the essentials! . . . Use every means to share Christ and invite people to salvation. (4) Most importantly, Repent! All of us and not just the worst of us need to respond to the challenges we face with repentance. Each of us must repent. In the words of a timeless hymn, 'All is vain unless the Spirit of the Holy One comes down.' God must move in us first, if He is to ever move in our churches. God will not bless those unpleasing to Him. We must become blessable or we will become expendable. We are the persistent hindrance to revival – all of us!*[98]

Is evangelism in the Southern Baptist Convention "gone with the wind"? It appears that it is, at least (and hopefully) temporarily, but we can certainly pray that the wind of the Holy Spirit will bring it back.

---

98   Kelley, Obit., p. 52-53

THE AGE OF APOSTASY

THERE ARE MANY THINGS THAT MILITATE against another Conservative Resurgence – subjectivism, pragmatism, relativism, pluralism, liberalism, egalitarianism, misappropriated priorities, a society that has become hostile to the Gospel - all designed and orchestrated by the devil. I have often thought that Southern Baptists were the last line of defense against the age of apostasy, but does the decline of the largest evangelical body in the nation indicate that we too are in the throes of the great "falling away."

BIBLICAL REVIVALS

Since the fall of Adam and Eve in the Garden of Eden, this world has been marked and marred by sin. In the days of Moses and Joshua the Israelites turned away from God and worshipped other gods. The era of the Judges in the Old Testament was characterized by political and military crises. However, when Samuel came on the scene, he called the people to repent, saying, "If you return to the Lord with all your hearts, then put away the foreign gods . . . and prepare your hearts for the Lord and serve Him only . . .He will deliver you" (I Samuel 7:3-4). God once again smiled upon Israel with favor and blessings.

Asa was the third king after Solomon and when he came to the throne in Jerusalem the nation was in turmoil because of idolatry, a lack of peace and trouble on every side. The people were living without the true God and without the true law. The Prophet Azariah spoke to Asa and said, "If you seek Him, He will be found by you; but if you forsake Him, He will forsake you" (II Chronicles 15:2). Asa obeyed the words of God through the prophet Azariah and "removed the abominable idols from all the land" and "restored the altar of the Lord". He also urged the people "to enter into a covenant to seek the Lord God of their fathers with all their heart and with all their soul" (II Chronicles 15:8, 12). There was a spiritual awakening in the land.

In Elijah's day, the Israelites had wandered away from God and turned to the worship of Baal. There was a famine in the land and the situation was desperate. However, as a result of Elijah's contest with the prophets of Baal on Mount Carmel, God proved Himself to be the sovereign God of might and majesty when he answered the prophet's prayer and send down fire from heaven. The children of Israel responded by shouting, "The Lord, He is God! The Lord, He is God!" (I Kings 18:39). A revival of religion brought forth showers of blessing literally and spiritually.

There are many other examples in the Bible of God rescuing an idolatrous and wicked people from danger and possible annihilation by virtue of a spiritual awakening. It happened in the days of Jonah, King Jehoshaphat, King Hezekiah, King Josiah, Haggai, Zechariah and Ezra. In the New Testament book of Acts we read about several revivals and amazing works of God, including the events at Pentecost (Acts 2-5) and the spiritual awakening of the Europeans as a result of Paul's second missionary journey in Acts 16:6-18:11. In every case God was at work delivering people from idolatry, wickedness and oppression and ushering in a season of spiritual refreshing.

REVIVALS THROUGHOUT HISTORY

In the 12th century the heretical papacy protected their hold on their religious beliefs with a vengeance. Those who failed to embrace all the teachings of the church were ostracized and often marked as dissidents. In the Alps of Italy and southeastern France, a devout group of Christians determined to remain true to the Word of God. Led by religious reformer, Peter Waldo, his followers developed an uncompromising allegiance to the Word of God. They became known as Waldensians and in later years a group of them came to North Carolina and founded the town of Valdese (the English version of Waldensians), which happens to be my hometown. But in 1184 the Waldensians, through the preaching of Waldo and the lay preachers he trained, spread the Gospel into Spain, Hungary, Switzerland and Flanders. A spiritual awakening occurred which resulted in "great evangelistic activity" and prompted "the Pope to attempt to crush them out and issue an edict calling for the immediate elimination of all heretics, and setting in motion the destruction of villages, cities, art, and culture in a way that would plunge Europe into the dark ages."[99] However, the spiritual impact of Peter Waldo and his band of believers continues to this day.

Then there was the Bohemian Revival of 1315, or the spiritual awakening led by John Wycliff and John Huss in the 14th century, as well as the movement of God in the 15th century led by Savonarola.

Later, Martin Luther was known as a great man of prayer; and as a result of his steadfast faith and uncompromising resolve, the Christian faith made a turn to the right that changed the course of human history. In the 16th century millions of souls continued to languish under the abusive leadership of the Roman Church, but history informs us that as Luther's prayers went up before God, and God came down to deliver people from the Catholic oppression.

Still later, John Calvin labored for 20 years to make Geneva a city known for its spiritual influence. In the beginning the city was known for its immodest clothing, dancing, taverns, "haunts of sin," and unchastity But after two decades of prayer and preaching the churches were filled to capacity and "Geneva became a fountainhead of Protestant inspiration to all Europe."

John Knox with his messages of "root and branch reform" brought a spiritual awakening to Scotland. In every case, lives were transformed, and cities and nations were liberated from the consequences of sin.[100]

---

99   https://www.project6000.com/english-home-page/30ac-b-our-salvation-and-tasks-are-coming-from-the-jew-yashua/12-13-cent-b--p-awakening-and-inquisition-in-southern-france/Accessed March 23, 2021

100   http://www.revival-library.org/revival_histories/evangelical/pre-1700/pre_1700.shtml/Accessed March 23, 2021

On Easter Sunday 1993, I asked Dr. Stephen Olford to preach for me. I was pastor of Peachtree Corners Baptist Church in the Atlanta area. He preached one of the greatest sermons I have ever heard. After the service my wife and I had the privilege of having Stephen and Heather Olford in our home for a meal. I had heard him say that he knew Evan Roberts personally. Roberts was one of the principal preachers in the Welsh revival in 1904. Dr. Olford said that prior to the revival, Wales was in trouble morally and spiritually. He said that the churches were empty and the taverns and brothels were filled with people seeking some temporary pleasure. Profanity was prolific and the nation was in a serious crisis.

However, people started praying and Roberts made the appeal for people to ask God to "Send the Holy Spirit for Jesus Sake." It was not long until spontaneous singing and weeping and worshiping would take place in homes, businesses and churches. A spiritual revival emerged without any money spent, any advertisement, commercials or posters telling where meetings were being held. Fishermen five miles out in the Irish Sea suddenly came under conviction without any Christian present and made their way back to shore, found a church or a preacher, seeking salvation as they testified concerning their experience on the sea. Approximately 70,000 were saved in the first two months, and over 100,000 during the course of the revival. The moral and spiritual trajectory of the nation was dramatically altered. After the revival, the taverns and brothels were out of business. Churches were filled to overflowing. Coal miners had cleaned up their profane language to the extent that they could not get their mules to pull the loaded wagons out of the coal mines, because the animals could not understand the sanitized language of the miners.

The First Great Awakening that occurred in the first half of the 18th century was aimed at a general sense of complacency among believers. According to multiple reports there was a spiritual dryness among those who professed to be saved. Religion became something of a pastime in which people would "go through the motions" during religious services without deeply felt convictions of the heart and soul. [101]

The Second Great Awakening dealt more with a moral slump than a spiritual dryness. One report indicates that drunkenness was epidemic.

Out of a population of five million, 300,000 were confirmed drunkards; they were burying fifteen thousand of them a year. Profanity was of the most shocking kind. For the first time in the history of the American settlement, women were afraid to go out at night for fear of assault. Bank robberies were a daily occurrence. The Methodists were losing more members than they were gaining. The Baptists said they had their most wintry season. The Presbyterians in general assembly deplored the nation's ungodliness. In a typical Congregational church, the Rev. Samuel Shepherd of Lennox, Massachusetts in sixteen years had not taken one young person into the fellowship. The Lutherans were so languishing that they discussed uniting with Episcopalians who were even worse off. . . The Chief Justice of the United States, John Marshall, wrote to the Bishop of Virginia, James Madison, that the Church 'was too far gone ever to be redeemed.' Voltaire averred, and Tom Paine echoed, 'Christianity will be forgotten in thirty years.'"[102]

101 http://www.great-awakening.com/basic-concepts-of-the-first-great-awakening/Accessed March 23, 2021

102 https://www.reviveourhearts.com/podcast/revive-our-hearts/role-

However, the Second Great Awakening resulted in thousands of souls being saved, a temperance movement launched, the abolition of slavery initiated, prison reforms enacted, and care for the handicapped and mentally ill undertaken. The awakening altered the moral and spiritual temperature of the nation. It even sought to implement Christian beliefs into national politics.

When any Christian culture begins to fail morally and spiritually you will generally find an impotent church that must bear culpability for the decline. When the church is weak it cannot be the restraining force to keep evil at bay. Its power is compromised. Its influence is negligible. Its message is diluted. Its voice is muffled. Its motives are suspect. Its mission is diverted. Its programs are ineffectual.

On the other hand, when churches are vibrant and experiencing revival the whole society in impacted. Souls are saved. Lives are transformed. Burdens are lifted. Drunkards are made sober. Harlots are made pure. Politicians are made honest. Marriages are made whole. Employees work harder. All ethnicities are in harmony. Satan trembles. The nation is spared and delivered from ruin.

There is so much at stake when the church begins to drift. It is no longer anchored by the Word of God, no longer zealous about reaching the lost, no longer an authentic representative of Christ in this world, and headed toward becoming apostate. And that kind of church is not comfortable hearing a bold, clear, authoritative, anointed message from a preacher or prophet of God.

-prayer-spiritual-awakening/Accessed March 23, 2021

JUDGMENT WILL BEGIN AT THE HOUSE OF GOD

The prophet Jeremiah stood in the gate of the Lord's house and pronounced a solemn curse. His announcement of judgment was not on the "enemies" of the Lord, but upon the people who were in the temple – the Jewish nation itself. The prophet thundered, "Amend your ways and your doings, and I will cause you to dwell in this place" (Jeremiah 7:3). Jeremiah was offering the people a promise, but it was based on the condition of the people changing the way they had been living. Jeremiah then boldly warned the people against trusting in lying words, stealing, murdering, committing adultery, telling lies, worshipping idols and walking after other gods (Jeremiah 7: 8). They were going to the temple to worship Jehovah, but that did not keep them from committing all these abominable sins. Jeremiah told the people they had made God's holy house "a den of thieves." In chapter 12 the question is asked, "Were they ashamed when they had committed abomination?" The answer comes back with the clarion sound of a trumpet: No! They were not at all ashamed, nor did they know how to blush (Jeremiah 8:12)

Those who professed to know God had become so wicked that God said to Jeremiah "Therefore do not pray for this people, nor lift up a cry or prayer for them, nor make intercession to Me; for I will not hear you" (Jeremiah 7:16). Jerry Vines, in his Expository Bible, indicates that it is possible that Jeremiah's message in chapter 26 could have occurred on the same occasion as the message in chapter 7. Vines writes, "If this is the same, then chapter 7 emphasizes the content of Jeremiah's message while this chapter (26) emphasizes the reaction of the people to the message."[103]

---

103 Jerry Vines, The Vines Expository Bible, (Thomas Nelson, Nashville, Tennessee 2018) p. 1101

And what was the reaction of the people? They cried out, "This man deserves to die! For he has prophesied against this city, as you have heard in your ears." Because Jeremiah had proclaimed the truth, the people were calling for a death sentence. How do you think people would respond today to Jeremiah's prophecy? I think they would attack him with animosity at worst and look at him askance at best.

I have made it a habit of basically memorizing my sermons for almost three decades. I will write out an entire manuscript and then go over it until it is implanted in my mind. That is not an easy task for me; and it takes hours of study, rehearsing and committing to memory my sermons. Once I have the sermon indelibly sketched into my memory, I try to internalize it and get it into my heart, because I have no desire to impress anyone with my ability to memorize a sermon, but I am very concerned about preaching from my heart with love and passion. My desire is not only to address the intellect but also the emotions of those who hear me preach because I want them to understand the seriousness of their sins, the necessity of being saved, and make sure the redeemed of the Lord are in step with God's will for their lives.

Several years ago, I decided I was going to try to memorize Jonathan Edwards sermon, "Sinners in the Hands of an Angry God." There was a church in Enfield, Connecticut that seemed to be unmoved by the call for a complete surrender to Christ. Edwards, was known for preaching sermons that aroused indolent believers and compelled the lost to see the tragedy of their hopeless condition, repent of their sins and be converted. Edwards was invited to preach at the Enfield church on July 8, 1741 at the height of the first Great Awakening. He selected Deuteronomy 32:35 as his text: "Their foot shall slide in due time." The text highlighted God's anger toward the wickedness and faithlessness of His people. We have been told that when Edwards preached that sermon there were people who held on to the pillars of the church for fear they were going to slip into perdition, others fainted, while yet others wept their way to the altar in penitential tears.[104]

To my own shame I must woefully admit that I never did much to commit "Sinners in the Hands of an Angry God" to memory for three reasons. First, when I realized the sermon exceeded 7,200 words and would require approximately one hour and 45 minutes to preach, I began to doubt that I would ever receive an invitation to preach it. Second, I also noted that Edwards' extraordinary vocabulary and phraseology would be difficult to master, because memorizing my own meager homiletical efforts is a sufficient challenge for someone my age. Third, As I read and reread the sermon, I seriously doubted that a 21st century congregation would have the spiritual receptivity to listen to a sermon depicting "the black clouds of God's wrath hanging over our heads and the glowing flames of the hell's fury licking at our feet."[105]

Earlier, I asked, "How do you think people would respond today to Jeremiah's prophecy?" My answer to the question is, "I don't think most church people today would respond well to Jeremiah's prophecy. It would most likely be a bit too harsh and pointed for them." If a preacher would stand in the church and decry the church's unfaithfulness, even pronounce God's judgment against it, he would very

104 https://www.enotes.com/topics/sinners-hands-an-angry-god/Accessed March 23, 2021

105 https://www.blueletterbible.org/comm/edwards_jonathan/sermons/sinners.cfm/Accessed March 23, 2021

likely be considered repugnant and offensive, even impolite and unseemly.

To decry the sins of a secular, decaying culture is one thing, but to condemn the sins of the church is unacceptable, particularly if you use the kind of language Jeremiah or Jonathan Edwards did. But we must understand that judgment begins "at the house of God" (I Peter 4:17). But I am convinced that the revivals and spiritual awakenings have temporarily stayed the hand of apostasy through the ages, but the closer we get to the rapture of the church, the closer we get to the full blown, godless, unrelenting age of apostasy that will bring about the awful tribulation described in Revelation 6-18.

We have already talked about the seeker-sensitive, felt-needs, consumer-friendly church goers who have become conditioned to mild, unobtrusive, appeasing sermons that do not offend. This is a sign of an apostate church. Paul wrote Timothy and said, "For the time will come when they will not endure sound doctrine, but according to their own desires, because they have itching ears, they will heap up for themselves teachers; and they will turn their ears away from the truth and be turned aside to fables" (II Timothy 4:3-4).

When we turn away from the truth, we become vulnerable to the seductions of those who work evil, we begin to believe the fake news that deceives and deludes, we begin to embrace the philosophies that are errant and injurious, and in all too many cases lead us down a primrose path to destruction. Christians are to be the salt of the earth and the light of the world. If salt loses its potency it is worthless and if a light is hidden from view the world is plunged into greater darkness (Matthew 5:13-16). Christians grow listless and lethargic. The church's influence wanes and weakens. The Bible is no longer regarded as infallible nor sufficient. The world is rife with restlessness and rebellion. The great apostasy is imminent.

AS APOSTATE CHURCH BREEDS AN IMMORAL SOCIETY

The apostasy in the churches of America did not happen quickly, but gradually, methodically, and unrelentingly. For almost 100 years we have seen God systematically removed from our society and when an action is taken to accomplish the purpose of evil, Christians have raised their voice in protest for a season, but then acquiesce to the enemy, relinquish the spiritual ground lost in that fight, retreat to their safe havens and hope their freedom in Christ will not be infringed upon again until the distant future. This has happened repeatedly in our culture as we have already noted in the ebb and flow of spiritual revivals in history. Every time a pastor or Bible teacher compromises the Word of God, every time a believer's profession is contradicted by his behavior, every time the church retreats one inch on ethical and moral issues, every time a Christian society pushes God to the periphery of the culture, the Bible's prophecies of an apostasy, a falling away becomes more of a reality. And while periods of spiritual decline have been partially rescued with seasons of spiritual renewal, the overall trajectory has been downward toward the apostasy described in II Thessalonians 2:3, I Timothy 4:1-2, II Timothy 4:3-4, II Timothy 3:1-5,7; I John 5:19, and Jude.

From the early 1600s to the late 1700s, Christianity, the Bible and creation were taught in America's schools. In 1749, Benjamin Franklin, in a booklet on education, said the teaching of history in schools "affords frequent opportunities of showing the necessity of a public religion . . . and the excellency of the Christian religion above all others."[106] In 1844, Daniel Webster, the famous "defender of the Constitution" argued before the Supreme Court that Christianity is inseparable from education."[107] However, with the passing of time, textbooks less favorable to Christian ideals were published. By the beginning of the 20th century, secular ideologies began to creep into the schools' curriculum and the Bible began to receive a minimal amount of attention. So, while the United States was founded with God as the centerpiece of our society, it has become increasingly apparent that He has been systematically pushed to the circumference over the years.

For example, to our peril, the theory of evolution eventually forced its way into our public school system, alleging that man was not made in the image of God, but in the image of animals. In order to put evolution on the throne and creation on the scaffold, the evolutionists must discredit the Bible as myth or poetry, not to be taken literally. Advocates of evolution essentially remove God from the creation equation and consequently, must conclude that man is the pinnacle of the evolutionary process and automatically usurps God's place in determining what is right and wrong. This thought process lends itself to the ideology of subjectivism discussed in chapter four. According to Answers in Genesis,

> *"Evolution provides the scientific orthodoxy for the philosophies of Marxism, fascism, racism, apartheid and*

---

106 Benjamin Franklin The Papers of Benjamin Franklin, (Leonard W. Labaree (Yale University Press, New Haven, Connecticut, 1961) vol. III, "Proposals Relating to the Education of Youth in Pennsylvania," 1749, p. 413

107 David Barton, Original Intent, (Wallbuilder Press, Aledo, Texas, 1996), p. 56

unbridled capitalism. On the other hand, creationists believe that God is the Master Architect and Designer of this universe and as the Creator decides what is right and wrong. Furthermore, biblical creationism conforms to the total thrust of Scripture as it is unfolded from Genesis to Revelation.[108]

Few things have contributed to the relentless march of apostasy in America more than the "theory" of evolution.

After the onslaught of evolution there has been a barrage of Supreme Court decisions that have given evidence of the advancement of apostasy and the banishment of God from our society. In 1962, the United States Supreme Court ruled in the Engel v. Vitale case that school-sponsored prayers in our public education system violated the First Amendment Establishment Clause. The 22-word generic prayer was rather innocuous, but incurred the wrath of Steven Engel, a Jewish man, who vehemently opposed the prayer: "Almighty God, we acknowledge our dependence upon Thee, and we beg Thy blessing upon us, our parents, our teachers and our country." There was an immediate public outrage from those who opposed the decision, but the angst of the protesters soon subsided and today is seldom mentioned. [109]

The following year, 1963, the Supreme Court made a landmark ruling in the Abington v. Schempp decision that declared Bible reading and prayers in public schools unconstitutional. Once again there was a brief season of dissent over the decision, but it soon vanished into the realm of convic-

---

108 https://answersingenesis.org/theistic-evolution/what-should-a--christian-think-about-evolution/Accessed March 23, 2021

109 https://www.mtsu.edu/first-amendment/article/665/engel-v-vitale/Accessed March 23, 2021

tional obscurity. In 2013, there was a significant number that gathered at the First Unitarian Church of Philadelphia with Ellery Schempp, who was by then a 72-year-old retired physicist, to celebrate the fifty-year anniversary of the high court's decision, one of several events observing the banning of Bibles in public schools. [110]

Madalyn O'Hare Murray, the infamous atheist, filed a lawsuit during the same time period which also contributed to the removal of compulsory Bible reading in public schools. And in 1965 the Supreme Court upheld a decision banning the voluntary recitation of a religious nursery prayer in public schools before eating cookies and milk each morning. The prayer referenced is "God is great, God is good, and we thank Him for our food."

The slide down the slippery slope of apostasy becomes increasingly precarious as the decades pass by; and the Roe v. Wade ruling of the Supreme Court in 1973 is a prime illustration of a declining culture. The landmark decision ruled (7-2) that the Constitution of the United States gives a woman the freedom to choose an abortion as protected by the privacy rights guaranteed by the Fourteenth Amendment to the U. S. Constitution. In making this decision legalizing abortion, the United States joined non-Christian countries like Nazi Germany, which promoted abortions for the purpose of so-called racial hygiene in 1935, Communist Russia, where abortion was legalized by the leader of the Red Terror, Vladimir Lenin, in 1920, and Japan, which has a record of induced abortions as early as the 12th century. [111]

---

110 https://www.theatlantic.com/national/archive/2013/06/50-years-
-after-i-abington-v-schempp-i-a-dissenter-looks-back-on-school-
-prayer/276921/Accessed March 23, 2021

111 https://en.wikipedia.org/wiki/Timeline_of_reproductive_rights_le-
gislation/Accessed March 23, 2021

With America joining these nations in legalizing abortion, it reminds me of Ezekiel's words to a rebellious nation long ago. The prophet said, "When you offer your gifts and make your sons pass through the fire, . . . You say, 'We will be like the Gentiles, like the families in other countries, . . .'" (Ezekiel 20:31-32). In this passage the people of Israel were rebuffing the goodness of God that had continually been their portion through the years and expressed a desire to be like other nations. Any country that claims to be a nation "under God" must expect to have laws and restrictions that reflect their faith. However, in America it appears that there are those who want no law to fetter their inclinations and limit their "rights". They begin to see Christianity as restrictive and tiresome. They begin to compare their existence with the lives of people in other lands and they seem to suffer from the comparison. They want rights without responsibilities, welfare without work, and liberty without laws.

In 1980 the growing influence of the secular society and the fading authority of the apostate church witnessed the restrictions imposed for posting copies of the Ten Commandments on public classroom walls. In *Stone v. Graham*, the Supreme Court ruled that posting the Ten Commandments on the walls of public-school classrooms violated the establishment clause of the First Amendment, because the purpose of the display was essentially religious.[112] Seven years later the march toward a secular society continued with the Supreme Court ruling that a 1981 Louisiana law mandating creation science instruction violated the legal principle of separation of church and state. The court explained that the Pelican State law "was clearly to advance the religious viewpoint that a

---

112 https://www.mtsu.edu/first-amendment/article/696/stone-v-
-graham/Accessed March 23, 2021

supernatural being created mankind" and that such instruction was no longer permissible. [113]

The *Obergefell v. Hodges* case in June 2015, resulted in the Supreme Court stating that the Fourteenth Amendment requires all states to grant same-sex marriages and honor same-sex marriages granted in other states. While the 5-4 ruling provided a long-sought victory for the gay rights movement, the court's decision was in direct opposition to the teaching of God's infallible and immutable Word.

Another giant step toward secularism and apostasy was taken by the Supreme Court on June 15, 2020, when a 6-3 ruling was made to give homosexual and transgendered persons all the rights provided by Title VII of the 1964 Civil Rights Act. Justice Clarence Thomas wrote the leading dissent, declaring that the majority of justices were "Sailing under a 'textualist flag', essentially pretending to remain true to the words of the statute but instead updating it 'to better reflect the current values of society.'"[114] That is precisely what happens in apostasy; governments and churches jettison the truth of God's Word for whatever seems expedient at the time.

Obviously, there are examples *ad infinitum* of our beloved nation forsaking our Christian heritage. There are those who want to remove "under God" from our pledge of allegiance to the U. S. flag. Others want to exclude "in God we trust" from our currency. Months ago, there were those who wanted to replace *The Star-Spangled Banner,* our national anthem, with John Lennon's song, *Imagine,* which would be very appropriate for the American Association for the Advancement of Atheism

113 https://www.latimes.com/archives/la-xpm-1987-06-20-mn-8487-story.html/Accessed March 23, 2021

114 https://www.npr.org/2020/06/15/863498848/supreme-court-delivers-major-victory-to-lgbtq-employees/Accessed March 23, 2021

or the Freedom From Religion Foundation. Furthermore, it has also been reported that all Christian symbols in Veteran Affairs chapels must be covered or removed in order to be maintained as "religiously neutral."[115]

SIGNS OF APOSTASY

While America is called a Christian nation, the evidence for that is becoming somewhat suspect. Today there are more atheists and agnostics than evangelical Christians in the United States. According to the Pew Research Center, 25.4 percent of adults in the U. S. identify with evangelical Protestantism. [116] The "nones", those who describe their religious identity as atheist, agnostic or 'nothing in particular,' now stands at 26 percent, up from 17 percent in 2009. [117]

How did this national "falling away" happen? Because, as we have already emphasized, the church, the saving salt, has lost its savor. Salt has always been a valuable commodity. NaCl2 has been used as a mark of friendship, to bind a covenant, give flavor, create thirst, and act as a preservative. Christians as individuals and the church as a body are to be a preserving influence in the world. When a nation is tending toward corruption, the church must aspire to be the sav-

115 https://www.jacksonville.com/article/20150808/NEWS/801250863/ Accessed March 23, 2021

116 https://www.pewresearch.org/fact-tank/2018/03/01/5-facts-about--u-s-evangelical-protestants/Accessed March 23, 2021

117 https://www.pewforum.org/2019/10/17/in-u-s-decline-of-christianity-continues-at-rapid-pace/Accessed March 23, 2021

ing salt to arrest the corruption and bring renewed life. John MacArthur, writes,

As a preserving influence, Christians are to retard moral and spiritual spoilage. When the church is taken out of the world at the rapture, Satan's perverse and wicked power will be unleased in an unprecedented way (see II Thessalonians 2:1-12). Evil will go wild and demons will be almost unbridled. Once God's people are removed it will take only seven years for the world to descend to the very pits of hellishness.[118]

Martyn Lloyd-Jones provides a marvelous example of Christians who became the preserving salt for the sake of England. He writes,

Most competent historians are agreed in saying that what undoubtedly saved England from a revolution such as that experienced in France at the end of the eighteenth century was nothing but the Evangelical revival. This was not because anything was done directly, but because masses of individuals had become Christians and were living this better life and had this higher outlook. The whole political situation was affected, and the great Acts of Parliament which were passed in the last century were mostly due to the fact that there were such large numbers of individual Christians found in the land.[119]

---

118 John MacArthur, The MacArthur New Testament Commentary, Matthew 1-7, (The Moody Bible Institute, Chicago, Illinois, 1985), p. 243

119 Martyn Lloyd-Jones, Studies on the Sermon on the Mount, (Eerdmans Press, Grand Rapids, Michigan,1971), p. 1:157

> **I DO NOT BELIEVE OUR PRIMARY PROBLEM TODAY IS INERRANCY, TODAY IT IS SUFFICIENCY.**

While the Conservative Resurgence in the Southern Baptist Convention most assuredly elevated a greater understanding and appreciation for the truth and infallibility of God's Word, and while it may also have temporarily held back the drift toward apostasy, it did not result in a sweeping, weeping, reaping revival across the nation. What is needed today is the full and unapologetic embracing of God's Word as infallible and sufficient; and a revival of Christianity in America that that will result in countless salvations and a spiritual overhaul of our churches and the educational, economic, social, entertainment and political entities of our society.

Southern Baptists may still become the saving salt for arresting the corruption of our nation, but it will take no small measure of devotion. We must give up the concept of thinking our battle is with flesh and blood. It is not! It is a spiritual battle and requires believers who are filled with the Spirit, have on the whole armor of God, and are steeped in prayer. And we must have a whole-hearted commitment to the truth of God's Word. The sufficiency of Holy Scripture is the critical issue at this point in our history. If we deny the sufficiency of God's Word our faith is shattered, our power is compromised, our prayers are ineffectual, our evangelism is flawed and our hope for victory is nullified, because the arm of flesh will fail us every time.

In the Conservative Resurgence the battle for the infallibility of the Bible was won; and today one would be hard pressed to find a Southern Baptist who blatantly denies the inerrancy of Scripture. But I do not believe our primary problem today is inerrancy, today it is sufficiency. On May 23, 1993

James Montgomery Boice celebrated his 25-year anniversary as pastor of Tenth Avenue Presbyterian Church in Philadelphia, Pennsylvania. In his sermon on that Sunday he asked,

> *Do we really believe that God has given us what we need in (His) Book? Or do we think we have to supplement the Bible with other man-made things? Do we need sociological techniques to do evangelism? Do we need psychology and psychiatry for Christian growth? Do we need extra-biblical signs or miracles for guidance? Is the Bible's teaching adequate for achieving social progress and reform?"*

Boice continued,

> *The reason I believe this is important is that it is possible to believe the Bible is the inerrant Word of God, the only infallible rule of faith and practice, and yet neglect it and effectually repudiate it just because we think that it is not great enough for today's tasks and that other things need to be brought in to supplement the revelations. I think this is exactly what many evangelicals and evangelical churches are doing."[120]*

Boice continued by emphasizing that the Word of God is sufficient for all times, in all places and for all purposes. Although the Tenth Avenue Presbyterian pastor preached that sermon twenty-eight years ago, he could have chosen Mike Stone's title "My Analytical Tool – the Bible" for his message.

---

120 https://www.tenth.org/resource-library/articles/the-sufficiency-of--the-word-of-god/Accessed March 23, 2021

THE ADVANCE OF SOCIALISM AND ITS SPAWN

In His book Saving Freedom: Can We Stop America's Slide into Socialism, former U. S. Senator Jim Demint, writes,

For (more than sixty) years America's federal government has been aggressively purging religion and religious-based values from our society." He explains that originally the scope and authority of the federal government was very limited, but over the years has crept outside its constitutional bounds until all aspects of American society are under the authority of the federal government including: "the air we breathe, the water we drink, the food we eat, the clothes we wear, the homes we live in, the fertilizer we put on our lawns, the phones we talk on, our jobs and businesses, our schools and colleges, the cars we drive, the roads we drive on, the gas we put in our cars, the electricity for our homes, our health care, our investments and retirement plans, how we raise our children, the words we speak . . . even our churches.[121]

Demint contends that the federal court's ruling in the *Engel v. Vitale* case began the process of separating God from public life in America and completely distorted the definition of the "church." That is what socialism does. Its tentacles are reaching into every area of our lives and making it impossible for freedom to work. Socialism is the greatest enemy of the Gospel in America. It is the goal of socialism to remove God from the culture and from the nation. The entry of socialism is

---

121   Jim Demint, Saving Freedom: We Can Stop America's Slide into Socialism (Fidelis Books, Nashville, Tennessee, 2009) p. 158

the exodus of religion. Socialist countries today are completely secular and are determined to root out Christianity. It is a religion of envy. Its scientific materialism and monism makes it totally incompatible with Christianity. Socialism is responsible for the growing number of non-believers in the United States.

In the course of these pages, we have considered several of the "isms" that Vance Havner, the great revivalist of another generation, said should be 'wasims'. However, socialism is the one additional "ism" that may be our biggest threat, because it dilutes, even undermines the Word of God. This ideology has almost permeated our society and has also successfully crept into our denomination. It may be our greatest threat and will surely hasten our "falling away" unless we rise up against it with a fervor and passion unparalleled in our convention's history.

Socialism could be our greatest enemy, because it spawns so many of the other destructive ideologies we have mentioned: Critical Race Theory, Intersectionality, Egalitarianism, LGBT advocacy, redistribution of wealth and rationalism most of which are pushing for acceptance in the church under the umbrella of social justice.

The issue of social justice has been magnified in our Convention to the extent that it has become a threat to the simplicity and clarity of the Gospel. In the 1960s and 1970s we were having to deal with the heresy of the social gospel, but today I believe we are having to confront both the heresies of the social gospel and social justice.

Allie Beth Stuckey, in a podcast sponsored by Prager U., says that many churches today preach that "the Lord is a God of social justice." She continued,

"You will find 130 references to "justice" in the Bible, but it is never preceded by the word "social", God cannot be the God of justice and social justice, because social justice is not just. Justice is getting what you deserve without favor, Social justice is getting what you don't deserve, because you are favored.

"Justice is blind; social justice is not. Let's say a man robs a store. Justice demands but one thing – that he be tried in a court of law and if he is found guilty, punished. That is not how social justice works. Social justice will not only seek to determine if a person is guilty, but attempt to discover his economic condition, learn about his upbringing (what kind of childhood did he have), about his race or ethnicity, (is he a member of a race or group that has been historically oppressed).

"Justice demands that everyone be equal under the law. Social justice demands that everyone be equal period – economically, socially, and in every other possible way. It all goes back to Karl Marx wanting to stir up the 'workers' against the 'capitalists' by promising a "workers" paradise that has never been created and by denigrating anyone and everyone who believes in God, democracy, capitalism, and civil discourse."[122]

Racism of any kind should be despised and condemned; and if we have been reconciled to God, we must be reconciled to one another regardless of race. I believe the deaths of George Floyd, Ahmaud Arbery, Breonna Taylor and others were tragic; and we should have joined the multitudes who mourned their deaths, but at the same time we need to

---

122 https://www.prageru.com/video/social-justice-isnt-justice/Accessed March 23, 2021

recognize that those untimely and unfortunate deaths precipitated a crisis in our nation. Rahm Emmanuel, former White House Chief of Staff and Mayor of Chicago, famously stated, "Never let a good crisis go to waste." We also need to remember that Hitler, Lenin and Mao were masters of using a crisis to lead their countries down the primrose path and over the cliff to destruction.

Because of social justice and allowing those who felt disenfranchised to protest with violence, the year 2020 was marked with chaos as cities like Portland, Seattle, Minneapolis, New York, Chicago and Atlanta were ravaged by riots and looting.

Years ago, Adrian Rogers preached a sermon in which he related a conversation that a reporter had with a young man who was participating in a riot. The reported asked, "What are you doing?

The rioter replied, "I am destroying the system."

"Why are you destroying the system?" inquired the reporter.

The young man, with a scowl on his face, answered, "I don't like the system?"

The reporter then asked, "What are you going to replace the system with?"

He said, "I don't know. We will figure that out later."

The reporter responded with great wisdom by saying, "Has it ever occurred to you, that those who incite you to riot, those who have challenged you, and in many cases paid you to destroy this system of government already know and have planned the type of government they want to put in place of this republic."

Satan has a plan to destroy everything that is good and godly in our churches and in our land. The answer to this dark day in which we live is not to march, loot and protest, but to turn on the light. The way to defeat the darkness of vain philosophies, foolish idolatry and the encroachment of apostasy is to preach the all-sufficient Gospel and tell people that the light of the world is Jesus.

GOD'S WORD IS SUFFICIENT

I often think of Paul's trip to Athens and his conversations with all the learned men of the city. In the midst of his debates and reasoning, you can be sure that the people of Greece heard the Word of the Lord, because Paul considered the Word of God altogether sufficient and completely adequate to reach the Thessalonians, the Bereans, and even the academically elite Athenians. He knew that the Word of God was superior to all of the ideologies and philosophies of those who were constantly debating their theories on Mars Hill and in the Areopagus.

Dr. Stephen Olford, has told the story of the man, back in the 1950s, who wanted to buy a Rolls Royce Silver Dawn automobile. The vehicle was a masterpiece of engineering and struck a perfect balance between beauty and power. Only 760 of those cars were made in the early 1950s and each one was exquisite. He asked a variety of questions about the innovative features of the car and the salesman answered each question in detail. But he could never get an answer about the horsepower of the car. Each time he asked that questions, the salesman proceeded to talk about another aspect of the Rolls Royce's design and craftsmanship. Finally, the prospective buyer came right out and asked, "Look, I am very interested in purchasing this car, but I want to know about the horsepower."

The salesman looked straight into the face of the man and said, "Sir, I can tell you in all sincerity – the horsepower is adequate." And so is the Word of God. It is sufficient. It is enough! If the Word of God is read, studied, believed on, lived out and preached fervently

IN MANY PLACES PREACHING IS BECOMING WATERED DOWN WITH HEAVY DOSES OF CULTURAL WISDOM, THERAPEUTIC ADVICE, PSYCHOBABBLE, MYSTICAL INTUITIONS, POSITIVE THINKING, AND POLITICAL AGENDAS, ALL MIXED TOGETHER WITH A BARRAGE OF SELF-HELP REMEDIES.

it can slow down the advance of apostasy in our land.

Unfortunately, today, we are seeing a strange departure from this once firm position of the sufficiency of Scripture. Nowhere is this more clearly seen than in the shrinking power of the evangelical pulpit. Trendy worship styles, worldly entertainment, crass pragmatism, pop psychology, and the like are all competing against the certainty of biblical exposition. In many places preaching is becoming watered down with heavy doses of cultural wisdom, therapeutic advice, psychobabble, mystical intuitions, positive thinking, and political agendas, all mixed together with a barrage of self-help remedies.

The 19th Psalm, which is a Psalm of David, is a monumental and concise statement regarding the sufficiency of Scripture. Listen to these words:

> "*The law of the Lord is perfect, converting the soul; The testimony of the Lord is sure, making wise the simple;*

The statutes of the Lord are right, rejoicing the heart;
The commandment of the Lord is pure, enlightening the
eyes; The fear of the Lord is clean, enduring forever; The
judgments of the Lord are true and righteous altoge-
ther" (Psalm 19:7-9).

The sufficiency of Scripture is the biblical teaching that the Bible is all the revelation that is needed to equip believers for Christian life and service. The Bible reveals who God is, who we are, our broken status before God, the way of redemption, and the way we are to live as those redeemed by God.

The poet John Greenleaf Whittier wrote these words:

We search the world for truth; we cull
The good, the pure, the beautiful,
From graven stone and written scroll,
From all old flower-fields of the soul;
As weary seekers of the best,
We come back laden from our quest,
To find that all the sages said
Is in the Book our mothers read[123]

The Apostle Paul needed only one weapon in his arsenal – the Word of God. The writer of Hebrews said, "For the word of God is quick (living) and powerful, and sharper than any two-edged sword, piercing even to the dividing asunder of soul and spirit, and of the joints and marrow, and is a discerner of the thoughts and intents of the heart."

---

123 https://www.poetrynook.com/poem/book-our-mothers-read/Accessed March 23, 2021

THE RISE AND FALL OF THE CONSERVATIVE RESURGENCE

What is going to happen to America?

Can we anticipate a genuine revival; or should we expect to see the church continue to decline and a deepening social degeneracy? God is immutable. He is the same yesterday, today and forever. His arm is not shortened that He cannot save. His Word is just as true and powerful as ever. However, there are many today who believe that in this age of apostasy the curtain is about to close on life as we have known it. There is an expectancy that Gabriel is licking his lips to blow the trumpet sounding the Lord's soon return.

Can we overcome the current spiritual morass, experience heaven-sent revival and have a rebirth of the Conservative Resurgence in the Southern Baptist Convention before Christ returns? I believe the Lord could very well use the Conservative Baptist Network to facilitate a rebirth of those principles and practices that make Southern Baptists the most formidable evangelical body in America.

"The CBN affirms the longstanding Baptist beliefs highlighted in the Baptist Faith and Message 2000. The Network is committed to the inerrancy, supremacy, and sufficiency of the Bible in all facets of life and application. This grassroots movement also affirms religious liberty and encourages Christian individuals and churches to influence the culture by engaging in the public policy process and demonstrating their patriotism. The CBN strongly believes in a just society for all based on biblical truth, opposing racism and sexism in all forms, and therefore rejects worldly ideologies infiltrating the Southern Baptist Convention, including Critical Race Theory, Intersectionality, and other unbiblical agendas deceptively labeled as "Social justice." The Network is committed to seeing the SBC function biblically – effi-

ciently and strategically –believing Convention entities and leadership are accountable to and encouraged by the autonomous, local churches that cooperate together."[124]

---

124 https://conservativebaptistnetwork.com/Accessed March 23, 2021

CHAPTER 8

THE OVERCOMERS

IS IT POSSIBLE TO BE ENCOURAGED AND HAVE hope for a spiritually renewed and energized Southern Baptist Convention? To be honest, I don't know. I know that God will always have a remnant and that there will always be surrendered saints who are on fire for God and faithfully obeying His will and fulfilling His Great Commission. But is there any Biblical promise or assurance that a great revival is coming with multitudes of people coming to faith in Christ and entire nations turning to the worship of the Lord? Since the Bible teaches that before Christ's return there will be a great "falling away" from the truth (II Thessalonians 2:3) and that the true church will become weak and have little strength (Revelations 3:8) will a genuine revival be possible before the rapture? It is a probing and piercing question.

The Bible teaches that in the last days, "The love of many will grow cold" (Matthew 24:12). Conscientious observers can see Christians who were once passionate about the things of God growing cold and indifferent. Many churches are just going through the motions and are so cold you could ice skate down the aisle, as one preacher famously quipped.

Another pastor, indicated that he has tried to picture the end coming like a glacier over the earth. He said,

"I don't know how fast it will come or whether it can come and recede, but I know it is coming. But I want to be a white-hot servant for Jesus when it comes; and wherever I'm speaking, wherever I'm living, wherever I'm pastoring, I am going to torch the glacier. I am going to poke up into the glacier and try to melt big holes in the glacier, so the glory of God comes shining through. Who knows? Perhaps enough churches poking holes in the glacier would make your city (or convention) a vibrant, white-hot witness and being found faithful when He comes."[125]

There are others, however, who firmly believe that a mighty revival is just over the horizon. They read Joel's prophecy about the "latter rain" mentioned in Joel 2:23 and interpret it to signify an end time revival and evangelistic harvest. In agriculture the farmer understands that right after a seed is planted an "early rain" is needed to cause the seed to germinate in order to produce a healthy crop. Periodic days of rain are also beneficial to the farmer's crop. But he also longs for a rain right before the harvest, which he refers to as the "latter

---

125 https://www.desiringgod.org/interviews/should-we-expect-revival-
-or-more-social-decay/Accessed March 23, 2021

rain", which can assure a high yield at harvest time. Those who hold to a "latter rain" theology teach that the Acts 2 outpouring of the Holy Spirit was the "early rain", but the "latter rain" will be an even greater outpouring of the Holy Spirit upon the church in order to prepare her for the great revival and harvest prior to Christ's return.[126]

However, I have not found any biblical evidence to indicate that there will be a great revival for the church as we draw near Christ's return. There are the warnings about apostate doctrine and moral decline and spiritual hypocrisy, but I have been hard pressed to find anything about a world-wide spiritual awakening. Nevertheless, I do believe in the sovereignty, omnipotence and grace of God and that He is free to send revival at any time He pleases. So, all that gives me a measure of hope.

Interestingly, another source of hope has come from a recent study of the first chapters of the book of Revelation. In chapters two and three we have the Lord's letters to the seven churches of Asia Minor. And Jesus Christ, the Lord of the Lampstands and the Christ of the Candlesticks writes a letter to these churches and gives them a report card, an evaluation.

WE SHALL OVERCOME

The first letter is to the church at Ephesus (Revelation 2:1-7). Christ is eminently qualified to be the appraiser, the judge of these churches. In Revelation 1:14 we are informed that His eyes are "like a flame of fire." That means that He is

---

126 https://core.ac.uk/download/pdf/58821983.pdf/Accessed March 23, 2021

not deceived by sham or pretense. He knows the good from the bad, the true from the false and that which is commendable from that which is contemptible. He begins by letting the Ephesian church know that they are to be blessed for their labor, their patience, their integrity and their ability to unmask the heresies and false religions of their day (Ephesians 2;2). However, the church had one overriding fault – they had lost their first love for Christ. It is not that they did not love, but the engagement, the precious love that a bridegroom has for his new bride was gone. Much of what they were doing was just by force of habit. They were mechanically going through the motions of worship and service, but there was no passion and no spiritual motivation. They were guilty of a sin no average person could see.

The Apostle Paul reminds us in I Corinthians 13 that if we have the ability to speak with eloquence, have the gift of prophecy, have all knowledge and the capability of unraveling the mysteries of the universe, possess great faith, give all our possessions to the poor and become a martyr, but have no love, it is all nothing more than a puff of wind on a dusty street. However, in spite of Ephesus losing their first love which likely created a faltering faith, uninspired labor and hypocritical worship, the Lord writes: "To him who overcomes I will give to eat from the tree of life, which is in the midst of the paradise of God" (Revelations 2:7) The tree of life is a sign of eternal life. It is in the midst of the paradise of God. The restoration of the Garden of Eden is in view as it is in Revelation 22:1-5. In Genesis, a flaming sword blocked the way to the tree of life, but he who overcomes will find it forever available. The Lord promised all resurrected believers to have access to the tree of life, in Heaven, and live forever. The promise is to those who overcome.

The second letter is to the church in Smyrna (Revelation 2:8-11). The Lord observes that this church is marked by her works, tribulation and poverty. Like the church at Ephesus, the church at Smyrna was a beehive of activity. They were rendering meaningful service in Jesus' name. In the midst of their service, they were suffering persecution. They had also lost their possessions, their social prestige and very likely any possibility of earning an honest living. The tribulation has produced poverty, but though they were poor in the things of this world, they were rich in spiritual growth and maturity. Yet in spite of their poverty and tribulation the Lord says, "He who overcomes shall not be hurt by the second death" (v. 11). In fact, the Lord promises them "the crown of life."

There are five crowns that Jesus will hand out to believers at the Judgment Seat of Christ. (1) The "crown of life", also known as the "martyr's crown" will be given to those who have endured persecution and trials for their faith even unto death. (2) In I Corinthians 9:25 the Apostle Paul speaks of the "imperishable crown" also known as the "victor's crown". This crown is for those who have run the race God assigned with faithfulness, who have kept their focus on Jesus and finished well. (3) The "crown of righteousness" mention in II Timothy 4:8 is for those who have lived righteously and served faithfully and who look forward with great anticipation to the Lord's return. (4) The "crown of rejoicing" mentioned in I Thessalonians 2:19-20 is the soul winner's crown. The Psalmist said, "He who continually goes forth weeping, bearing precious seed for sowing, shall doubtless come again with rejoicing, bringing his sheaves with him." Nothing should thrill the believer more than seeing someone rescued from the shackles of sin and set free by the saving grace of Christ, our Lord. (5) The "crown of glory" is the reward reserved for those who have been called by God to preach and teach His Word and who have lovingly cared for the flock of God during the absence of the Chief Shepherd.

Smyrna may have known physical persecution and the loss of all material possessions, but the Lord assured them if they would overcome, they would receive their just reward – a crown of life.

The third letter was written to the church at Pergamos (Revelation 2:12-17). The Lord blessed those at Pergamos who were dwelling in the shadow of Satan's throne and remaining faithful to His name. One of their own, Antipas, died as a martyr while still holding publicly to the name of Jesus. However, while there were those who held on to their faith in Christ, there were others who had become spiritually careless or permissive regarding the pagan influences; and there were sins that threatened the very life of the church. Some were guilty of holding on to "the doctrine of Balaam and the Nicolaitans" and others were engaged in "sexual immorality".

Once again, the Lord uses the word "overcome". This time it is given to a compromising church if they will repent. They are promised "hidden manna to eat". God provided manna for the children of Israel during their wilderness wanderings, but in Exodus 16:15, "Moses said to them, 'This is the bread which the Lord has given you to eat." Manna is one of the culinary delights the Lord will prepare for His saints in heaven. Those who overcome in Pergamos will also be given a "white stone". It is believed that in the Old Testament days, if someone was found guilty in a court of law, he would be given a black stone; if an individual was being tried for some crime and found not guilty, he would be given a "white stone". Every believer in heaven will be given a white stone indicating that their sins were washed away by the blood of Jesus.

The fourth letter was written to the church at Thyatira (Revelation 2: 18-29). The Lord looked at this church with "eyes like a flame of fire" and found some positive things to say about her. He commended the church at Thyatira for her works which were more zealously accomplished and effectively wrought at the end than at the beginning. He also praised the church for her love, service, faith and patience. It is interesting to contrast Thyatira and Ephesus. Ephesus was intolerant of evil but was deficient in love. Thyatira was growing in love but tolerating evil. Thyatira must have been like churches today that preach love and tolerance but seem to have difficulty in judging between good and evil. Good and evil cannot coexist, because the Bible explains that the righteousness has no fellowship with unrighteousness (II Corinthians 6:14). The compromise and duplicity in the church results in Jesus lowering the boom and condemning the church for tolerating Jezebel who has enticed some of them "to commit sexual immorality and eat things sacrificed to idols". Jezebel is perhaps the most notoriously conniving, treacherous, wicked woman mentioned in the Bible. She has become known as the epidemy of evil. No one names their daughters Jezebel. It is a name of infamy.

However, in verse 26 he offers them the opportunity to overcome and promises that He will give them" power over the nations" and "the morning star". When Jesus returns to the earth at the end of the tribulation period, and establishes His millennial kingdom, those in Thyatira who remain faithful to the end will rule and reign with Him over all the earth. Furthermore, they will be given Jesus, who is described in Revelation 22:16 as "the root and the offspring of David, and the bright and morning star." Thyatira was submerged in a world of darkness and yet, to the spiritually awakened and the overcomers Christ appears as the "morning light".

The fifth letter is to the church in Sardis (Revelation 3:1-6). Anyone looking for something for which to commend this church would probably have no more success than a blind man looking for a black cat in a coal mine. Sardis was disreputably known by the world as an "alive" church. After all, she had all the outward characteristics of a living, vibrant church as far as the world was concerned. In reality, however, she was as dead as a government job at four o'clock. As a "has-been" church, her best days were in the past. Jesus warns them of His imminent return and informs them that if they fail to watch, He will come suddenly, and they will either be ashamed or doomed. However, there is a slight glimmer of hope even for Sardis for Christ tells them to "wake up and strengthen the things that remain, that are ready to die". The church is on life support, but there is still the slim possibility of rejuvenation. There are a "few" people who have kept the faith and remained untainted by sin and will be marked as those who have made their robes white in the blood of the Lamb. In every generation God always has a remnant – a "few" people who will not bow their knee to Baal, a Noah here and a Daniel there and a Job over there. Perhaps it is for the sake of the few that the Lord issues an expression of hope.

Even to this dead, defeated, depressing church Jesus provides a life raft, an opportunity to overcome. To the church at Sardis the Lord says, "He who overcomes shall be clothed in white garments, and I will not blot out his name from the Book of Life; but I will confess his name before My Father and before His angels" (v.5). In Revelation 20:12 two different books are found in Heaven. One book records all human beings who have been physically born and whether or not they are alive or deceased. The other book records the names of the persons who have trusted Jesus to save them. Jesus is saying that all believers will be announced as children of God before the Heavenly Father and to all the angels that dwell there. This illustrates the longsuffering of God and shows that He is not willing for any to perish.

The sixth letter is to the church at Philadelphia (Revelation 3:7-13).

This is actually the only church that the Lord is able to bless without reservation or qualification. Some scholars believe the Philadelphia church represents the church age from 1700 to 1900, the time of the Great Awakenings where revivals were held; and many people were saved in America and Europe. This is the missionary church, the church of the open door. This church had made a commitment to believe the Word of God and obey the Word of God. They were also unashamed of the Lord Jesus Christ and openly proclaimed the Gospel both near and far. I found it interesting that the Philadelphian church has opposition from the false church, the synagogue of Satan (v.9). The true and faithful church will always have opposition because, as you remember, the devil never contends for that which is not worthwhile. He will attack the growing, thriving, spiritual-filled church. But God intervenes in the Philadelphian-like churches, and promises to bring their opposers to worship before their feet. The false church may have popularity and influence, but the day will come when they will have to bow to the faithful few who will proclaim the Gospel to the world.

The Lord promises that if the Philadelphia church overcomes, He will make them "pillar(s) in the temple of My God". Pillars are important because they hold up the roof of a marble or stone building. Entire buildings can be destroyed when pillars are dislodged, as in Samson's day when he removed the two middle columns in the Temple of Dagon. The Lord is saying, "There will never be a time when any Christian will be removed from the body of Christ."

The seventh letter is to the church at Laodicea (Revelation 3:7-13). This is the lukewarm church that nauseates God. I believe we are living in the age of the Laodicean Church today. This church is half-hearted about its worship, its service, its evangelism, its missionary enterprise and its ministries. They boast about being "rich, increased in goods and in need of nothing". I have been to some of the great cathedrals in Europe and many of them, though architecturally fascinating and incredibly beautiful, are little more than museums and tourist attractions. In America there are many churches that seem to be satisfied with their material wealth, but they are destitute in regard to their worship, evangelism and missionary outreach, and may very well become nothing more than a museum in some future day.

Jesus countered their evaluation of themselves by saying, "(You) do not know that you are wretched, miserable, poor, blind and naked" (v. 17). But even to this church that was too hot to be cold and too cold to be hot and was so distasteful to God that he wanted to "vomit" them out of His mouth, He offered the opportunity to overcome. This church has essentially excommunicated Christ. He is knocking on the church door from the outside trying to gain entrance. His desire is to sup with them. Interestingly, the Greek word used here for "sup" is "*diepnon*" which is the evening meal. In the Near East in Jesus day, breakfast was a very small meal often consisting of bread and something to drink, the noon meal was eaten in passing, but the evening meal was eaten in courses and was a time for lingering long at the table and having good fellowship. It is this kind of meal that Jesus was offering; and the offer included the privilege of sitting down with Jesus on His throne.

The promises to those who overcome are lavish, loving and lasting, but it is nothing more than amazing grace that God would offer a loveless church like Ephesus, a poverty-stricken church like Smyrna, a compromising church like Pergamos, a Jezebel-friendly church like Thyatira, a dead church like Sardis and a lukewarm church like Laodicea the opportunity to overcome. If God would be so gracious to do that to the churches of Asia Minor, we need to pray that today He would look upon us as believers, as churches and as a beloved convention with favor and give the opportunity to overcome once again.

MORISON AND SUPLITA

There are many examples of God providing overcoming grace and salvation to faltering churches and hardened unbelievers, because they were willing to test the truth, follow the facts and obey the only One who could rescue them from disaster and doom. I think of Albert Henry Ross (pseudonym Frank Morison, 1881-1950), an Englishmen and a professed atheist, who set out to prove that the resurrection of Christ was a hoax. Morison was convinced that miracles do not happen and that the record of Jesus was nothing more than a good story. He decided to take his talent at writing, his keen scientific mind, and put them to work in order to untangle the cobweb of stories being told in the Gospels along with all available historical documents and prove once and for all that dead men simply do not rise again. Morison was convinced he could debunk the risen Christ and intended to call his book Jesus: The Last Phase. However, the more he read and the more intensive his research, the more he became convinced that his original premise was terribly wrong and at the conclusion of his writing he was brought to, what he called, "the unexpected shores of salvation." The book was titled Who Moved the Stone? [127] It was first published in 1930, but has been reprinted multiple times, most recently in 2006; and many people have been saved after reading the book.

In the preface of his book Morison writes,

> *The book as it was originally planned was left high and dry, like those Thames barges when the great river goes out to meet the incoming sea. The writer discovered one day that not only could he no longer write the book as he had once conceived it, but that he would not if he could.*"

He concluded the book by writing,

> *There may be, and, and the writer thinks, there certainly is, a deep and profoundly historical basis from that much disputed sentence in the Apostles' Creed "the third day He rose from the dead."* [128]

I love the story of overcomers and the following story illustrates God's grace and power to change any individual who will honestly seek the truth. In November 2011, I went to the University of Georgia to write a story on "The Great Exchange" for *The Christian Index*. The University has what is called "The Free Speech Zone" near UGA's Tate Student Center and anyone can reserve it to present their message or ideology. It is like the Areopolis in Athens.

---

127 https://jamesbishopblog.com/2016/03/08/atheist-frank-tried-to--debunk-christ-and-converted-instead/Accessed March 23, 2021

128 https://www.gospeltruth.net/whomovedthestone.htm/Accessed March 23, 2021

The college ministry of First Baptist Church of Watkinsville reserved the Free Speech Zone for the day and spent hours sharing the Gospel through the music of a praise band, testimonies and personal witnessing. At one point a man in his late forties appeared near the platform where the praise band was performing and he held up a sign that said, "Ask an Atheist." I discovered later that he was a psychology lecturer at the University of Georgia and was the faculty advisor for the campus atheist organization. Their motto is "Being Good Dawgs Without God." Dr. Suplita was offering what he considered a better alternative than Christianity and leading students to embrace a godless ideology.

I went back to the University the following spring and Dr. Suplita was there again, but this time he was passing out New Testaments and C. S. Lewis' book *Mere Christianity.* I was astonished at what I was witnessing, but I soon discovered that some of the men at First Baptist Church of Watkinsville had taken him on as a project and urged him to read the Gospel of John and the Epistle to the Romans. They began to mentor him and share their faith with him and after a few months he was glorious saved. He told me,

> *Last year at this time, I was convinced that atheism was true, but I couldn't deny or explain away the transformed lives of some of the people I knew who had embraced faith in Christ. I started listening for God to speak to me."*

Dr. Rich Suplita left the faculty of UGA and took up studies at Luther Rice Seminary, earned a master's degree in Christian Apologetics and is currently in a full-time ministry seeking to evangelize students at the university and discipling them in the Christian faith. On his website he says, "If He saved me, He can save anybody." On his Facebook page he has these words, "Come one! Come all! Come with your toughest questions! Christianity can stand the test of reason and "trial by fire" better than literally ANY other worldview!" Dr. Suplita's story is a clear testimony of God's saving grace and the sufficiency of God's infallible Word.

So, if God can save a skeptic like Frank Morison and an atheist like Dr. Rich Suplita we can be assured that He is still in the business of rescuing the perishing and redeeming recalcitrant sinners. Isaiah reminds us that "The Lord's hand is not shortened that it cannot save, nor His ear heavy that it cannot hear" (Isaiah 59:1). I believe God is saving people in proportion to our soul winning efforts. We were seeing far more people come to faith in Christ when our churches were investing much time, effort and financial support in personal soul winning, outreach ministries, revivals, Vacation Bible Schools, etc. As I have already mentioned, reaching the lost takes strong pastoral leadership, intentionality, focus, community penetration, financial support, membership involvement and especially tears and prayer.

GOD'S PROMISES ARE STILL VALID

In the previous chapter we outlined some of the greatest spiritual awakenings of the past, but must they remain as nothing more than the ashes of a once glorious history. I admit that sometimes I feel like Abraham who stood before the Lord and interceded for godless Sodom until divine grace was exhausted, but then I begin to recall the promises of God. He said, "Call to Me, and I will answer you, and show you great and mighty things, which you do not know" (Jeremiah 33:3). Jesus said, "Most assuredly, I say to you, he who believes in Me, the works that I do he will do also; and greater works then these he will do, because I go to My Father. And whatever you ask in my name, that I will do, that the Father may be glorified in the Son. If you ask anything in My name, I will do it" (John 14: 12-14). There are many others, but II Chronicles 7:14 seems to be the prescription for revival. "If My people who are called by My name will humble themselves, and pray and seek My face, and turn from their wicked ways, then I will hear from heaven and will forgive their sin and heal their land."

Our problem is that we are far more interested in the results of revival than the conditions for revival. Even in this age of apostasy, we may be able to have one more revival if we meet those conditions. The question is: are we willing to pay the price?

President Eisenhower once declared, "A soldier's pack may be heavy, but it is lighter than a prisoner's chains."[129] Paying the price of revival is far better than wearing the shackles of a godless regime. If you study the history of the great revivals and review the lives of the faithful men and the praying women who were the catalyst for those revivals you will discover that they agonized unrelentingly, humbled themselves selflessly, sought the Lord tenaciously, and repented so thoroughly that they often lay exhausted in a pool of tears. We reverence their memories, build them monuments and sing their praises. It is time we started to emulate their examples.

II Chronicles 7:14 prescribes humility if we want to have a spiritual resurgence. If we want to see our lives, our

---

129 https://www.eisenhowerlibrary.gov/eisenhowers/quotes/Accessed March 23, 2021

churches and our convention renewed, revived and restored we must first humble ourselves before God. There must be no selfishness, no hierarchy, no feeling of superiority, no spirit of rivalry, no racism, no prejudice, no hypocrisy, no pride among us if we are to have a denominational awakening. I want to be the first one to bow before the Lord and say, "God, be merciful to me, a sinner." I want to seek God with all my heart; and I know that the Psalmist said, "The wicked, in his proud countenance, does not seek God: God is in none of his thoughts" (Psalm 10:4). I do not want my life to be crippled by pride and I want God to dominate all my thoughts.

Prescription number two is prayer and specifically seeking the face of God. I believe there are three levels of prayer: (1) petition, when we ask God to meet our needs according to His riches in glory by Christ Jesus. (2) Intercession, when we lose sight of ourselves and pray for others as did Moses in Exodus 32:31-32 and Paul in Romans 9:1-3. (3) Communion is the highest level of prayer, because this is when we pray not for our needs to be met or for the needs of others, but when we pray simply to cultivate an intimacy with God. The Scripture stresses praying and seeking not God's hand, but God's face. When we get to the place of achieving that kind of understanding and affection, I believe we will have met that second requirement for revival and restoration.

Prescription number three is repentance or turning. Before there can be revival there must be renunciation. Sinful things must be forsaken. Doubtful things must relinquished. Review the confessional prayer of David in Psalm 51 and consider the consequences of his sin and the thoroughness of his confession. His turning from sin was apparently so complete that he was considered a man after God's own heart (I Samuel 13:14 and Acts 13:22). After his repentance David became known as a man who was committed to God's Word, God's will and God's ways.

So, is it possible for the Southern Baptist Convention to have a new spiritual resurgence? Absolutely! It won't be easy. In fact, it will be more difficult than the Conservative Resurgence nearly a half century ago. A new resurgence will occur in proportion to how committed we are to the prescription above.

Trust Publishers House,
the trusted name in quality Christian books.

Trust House Publishers
PO Box 3181
Taos, NM 87571

TrustHousePublishers.com